The Ultimate Guide to Syncopation: Concepts for the Development of Motion, Melody and Independence

By Bruce Becker

Layout by Tim Carman

Video Download

To download video:
Go to: halleonard.com/mylibrary
Enter code: **3578-1375-0672-6359**

This book is dedicated to all my students past and present!

Thank you to... Tim Carman, Jeffrey Smith, Keith Larsen, Rob Wallis, Jared Falk, Dave Atkinson, Mark Schulman, Jake Slichter and Steve Hatfield. Thank you to my teachers Freddie Gruber, Jim Chapin and Jerry Steinholz for the continued inspiration.

Bruce at Drumeo

www.instagram.com/brucebeckerdrums

www.youtube.com/brucebeckerdrums

TABLE OF CONTENTS

The Ultimate Guide to Syncopation

In my 50 years of Drumming and my 40 years of teaching, there is one book that remains a constant in my world, Ted Reed's Syncopation. I would always ponder, "Did Ted really know what impact his book would have on the Drum community?" It has consistently been in the top 10 of all time Drum Method books. The possibilities are endless.

In this presentation I want to offer some of the systems that I use in my teachings. Commonly, I see mostly page 33-44 [Older Printing] or 34-45 [Newer printing] being the "heart" of the book. Some of these systems you might be familiar with and others I hope to add a fresh look. I also include some interesting interpretations into other sections of the book that I use for important building blocks. As in the case of many of my favorite books that I've used, it is easy to feel overwhelmed by the content. I have my favorite individual exercises in each section and give highlights to bring forward each concept. My overriding advice and thought process is, that it is more important to embrace the "Concept" and not get overwhelmed by the Content. In other words, you don't need to do every single exercise but embrace each section and practice a few of these to allow the development of these concepts to permeate your playing. You can do a deep dive as you gain more comfortability. Whether it is for Rolls, Movement or Time concepts, it's all there.

I hope you enjoy some of these challenging and stabilizing exercises. Peace!

Bruce

Drum Key:

SECTION 1: The Rolls

In a quest to find a user friendly book that covers many potential concepts for Rolls I found many uses for earlier pages in Syncopation. One of my favorite uses is to help develop an easy relationship with Rolls and how the choreography enhances the "dance" of the Rolls. These moves are the starting point and I have adapted my value of movement to enhance how the Rolls move effectively and efficiently. These pages include 14-17 & 20-29. While there are other ways and movements that can be applied I have specifically set forward a path to develop an "Inner Logic" of movement. Once you are familiar and have the fundamentals that I have set forth as a natural reflex, see how more fluid your rolls feel. Be creative! Your ideas and additions are welcomed.

Developing the Motion for Triplet Based Rolls

Starting with pages 14 - 17 is a great way to breakdown the triplet based 7 stroke roll.
My begininng point for these is setting up the Triplets and identifying each 8th note triplet as a double stroke:

Here is an example of the move: using Page 14 #1.

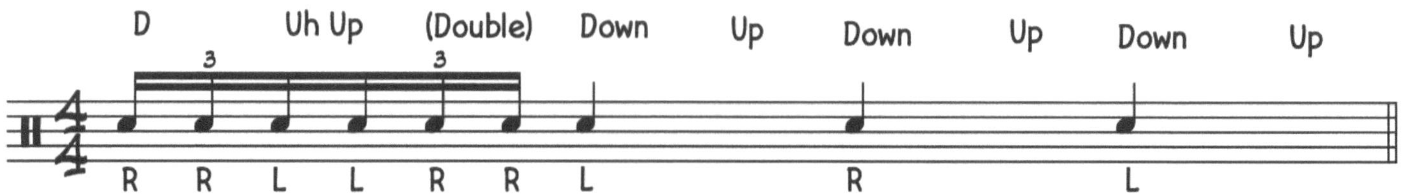

By using the flow of Upstrokes you can fine tune space and elasticity to create a fluid delivery. Remember the direction of the stick does not necessarily dictate the dynamic level. You can develop "touch" on a Downstroke and not allow gravity to sucker punch you into an accent. Also on the Upstroke you can fulfill a nice, dense accented stroke as well, and not get, as I always say..."a tippy tappy stroke". The position and timing of your stick and Upstroke are crucial in producing a full bodied stroke, but not overplaying it! A Tapstroke as well can be given a quality of density to the stroke to always add an equality to dynamics. Keeping this value of touch and density in mind is one of the keys in developing and enhancing your tonal quality. The redundancy of these moves will bring greater clarity and value as you go through these exercises. I have designed these to play slowly to give a greater feel for the 'flow"! The identity of these moves would also be represented in rudimental books like Wilcoxon's "All American Drummer". Remember it's "Concept" not "Content". Therefore, it is not necessary to do every single exercise. But make no mistake it is in your best interest to "know the difference" before moving on. You can make greater progress by focusing on these details and, by breathing into these lifts and drops you will add depth to your internal relationship to time!

Here are a few examples of selected exercises from Pages 14 - 17. When practicing these use a Metronome and drop your heels. When possible play on snare with BD on quarters and HH on "ans".

Page 14

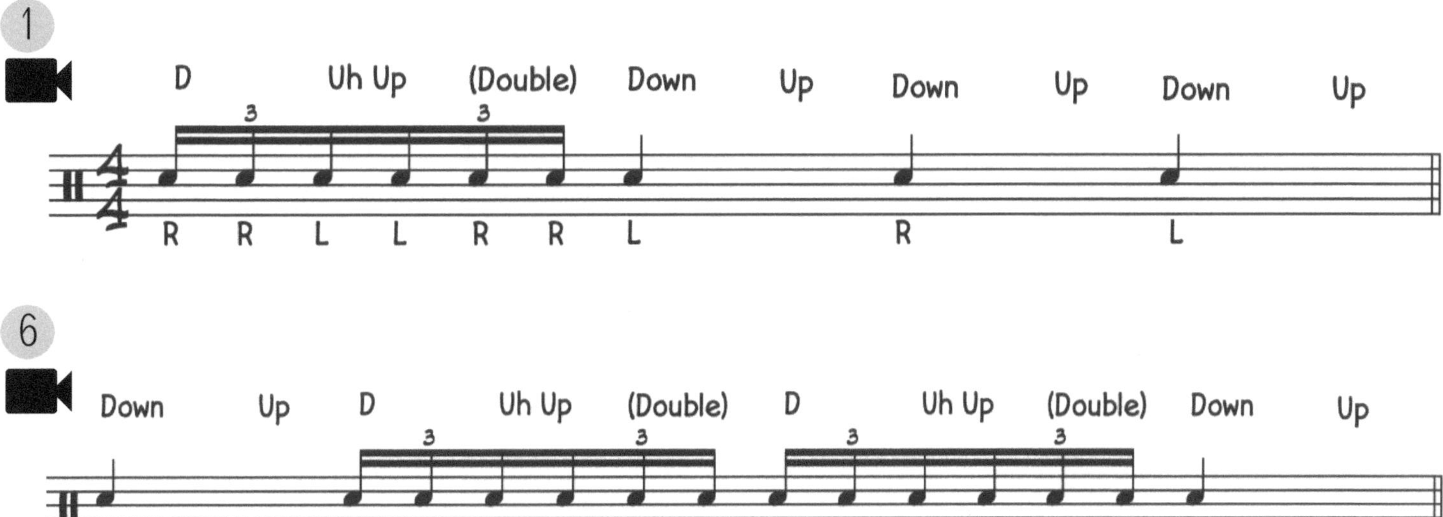

Page 15

15

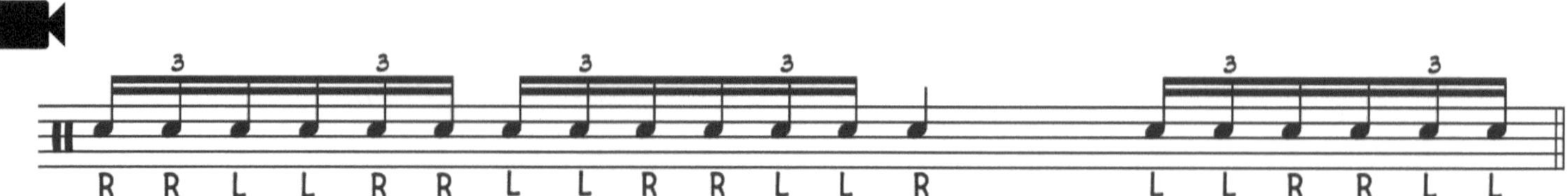

The 16 Bar Exercise on page 15: Right Lead and Left Hand Lead

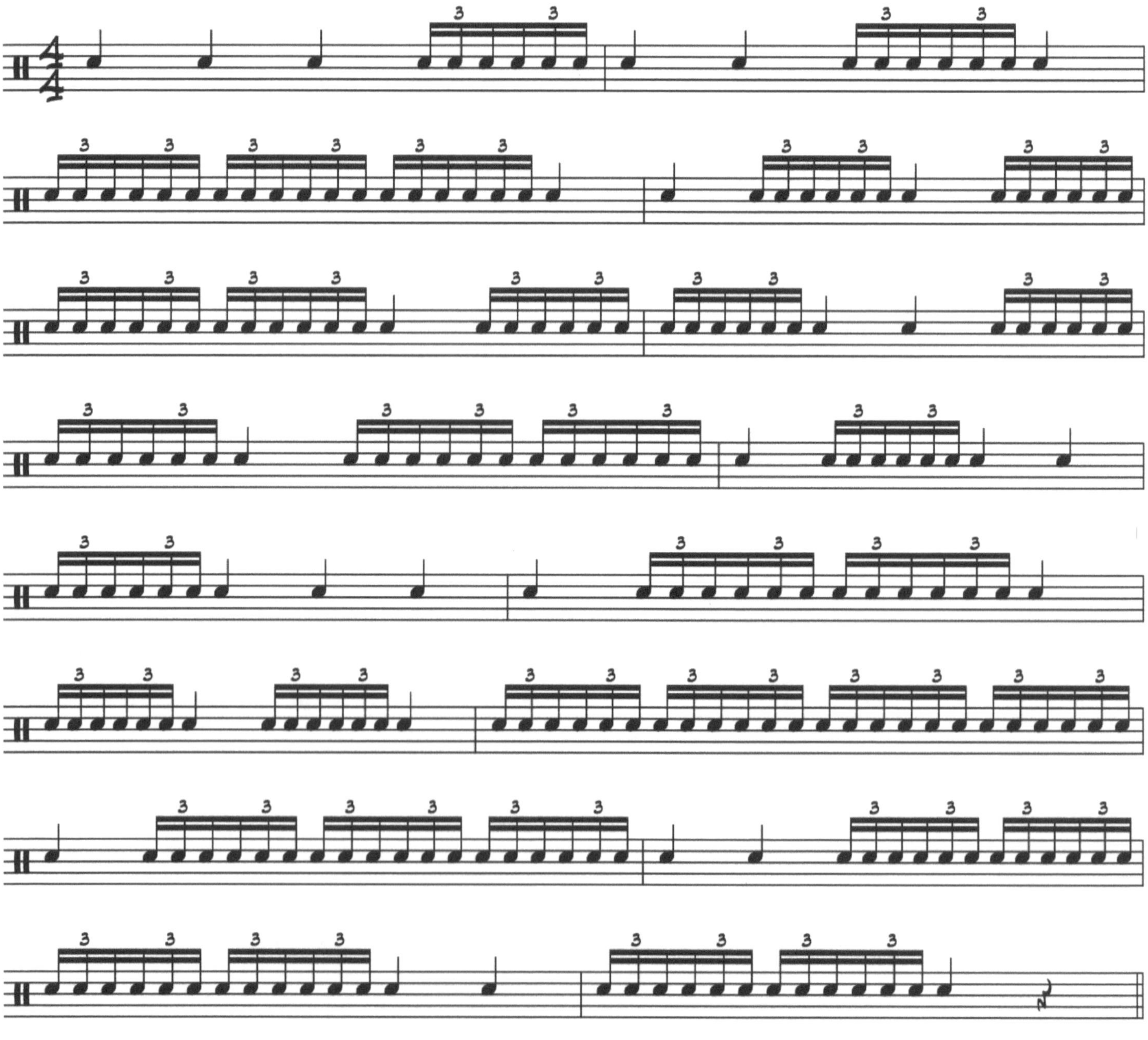

On Pages 16 & 17

There are 8th notes in the mix, so a Tapstroke will be added to the movement with the 8th notes. Here is an example of the choreography for a series of 8th notes. Again keep your attention on the movement and listen for your dynamics. Work on bringing a roundness to the phrasing.

8th Note EXAMPLE.

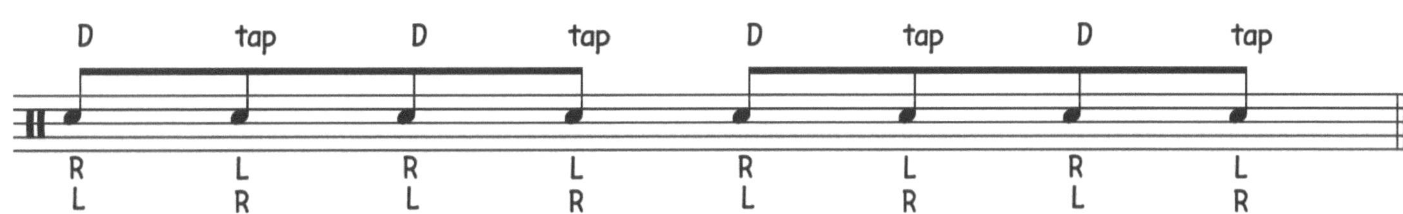

Now let's take a look at selected examples from Pages 16 & 17.

As you play this first exercise notice that you will alternate the roll each bar. Breath and play slowly! Recommended tempo: quarter note = 52

1

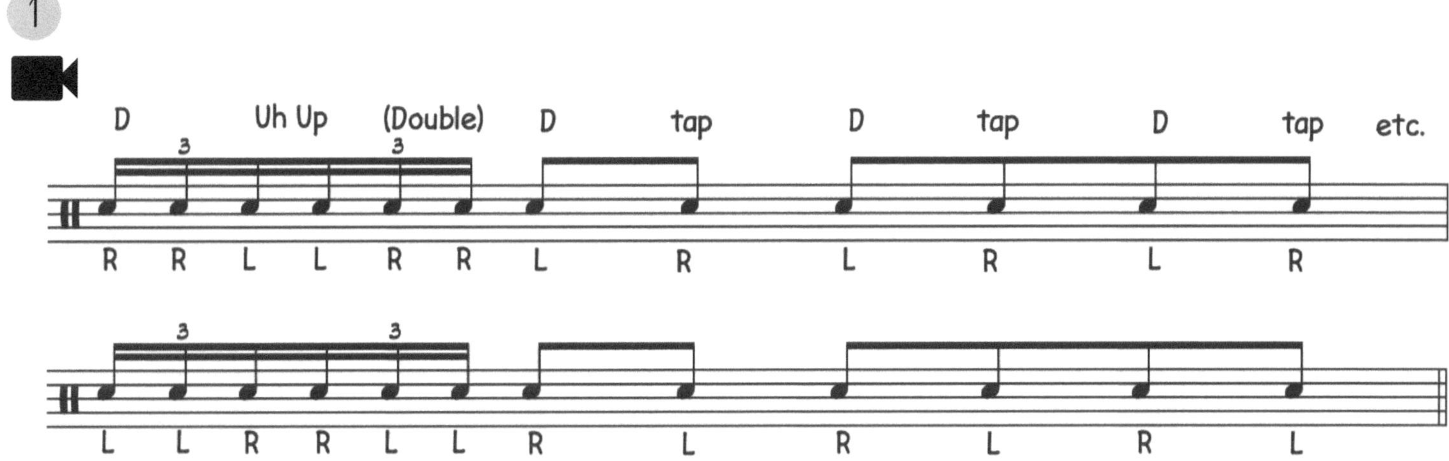

5

Page 16 and 17 continued

The 16 Bar exercise on page 17

As you play the 16 bar exercise notice that after a few bars you won't know which hand you started with. You get an equal distribution of RH leading rolls as well as LH leading rolls.

Developing the Motion for 16th Note Based Rolls

Continuing onward to Pages 20-29

I use these pages to develop the 16th note based rolls, i.e., 5, 9, 13 & 17 stroke rolls etc. Again these exercises will be increasing the value of choreography to bring fluidity to these rolls. The same theme from Pages 14 - 17 will be applied. Here is an Example from Page 20 to breakdown the outline of the 16th note Rolls. Remember to bring a fluidity to the Up strokes to produce a quality landing on the "Down".

The set up for the 16th Note based rolls:

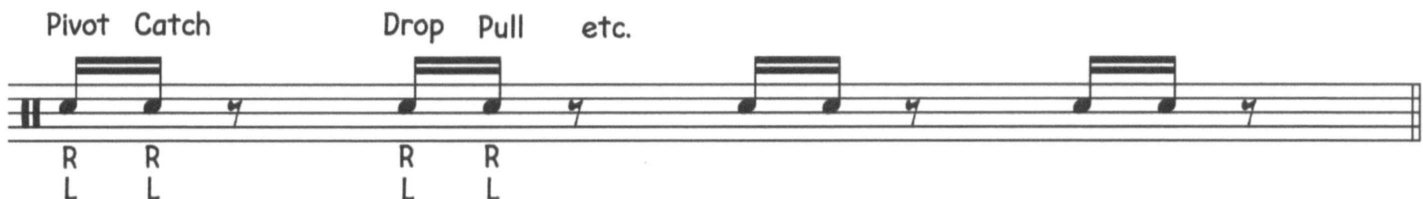

Then:

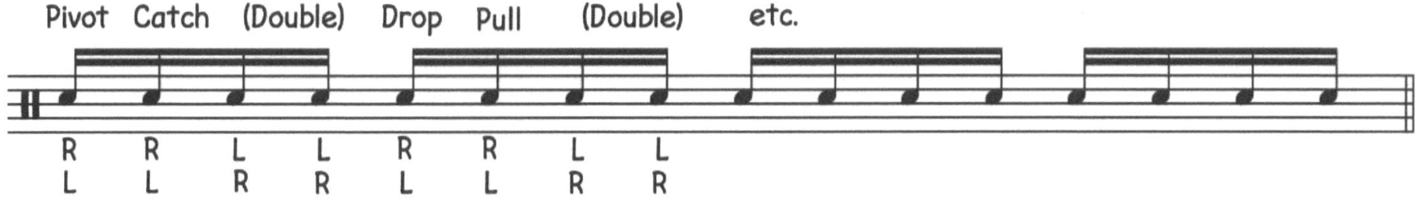

Apply to:

Here is an Example from Page 20 to breakdown the outline of the 16th note Rolls. Remember to bring fluidity to the Upstrokes to produce a quality landing on the Down. Drop your heels when playing on the pad. When on the drum set, play 1-2-3-4 on the BD and 2 & 4 on the HH.

Here are some more selected examples:

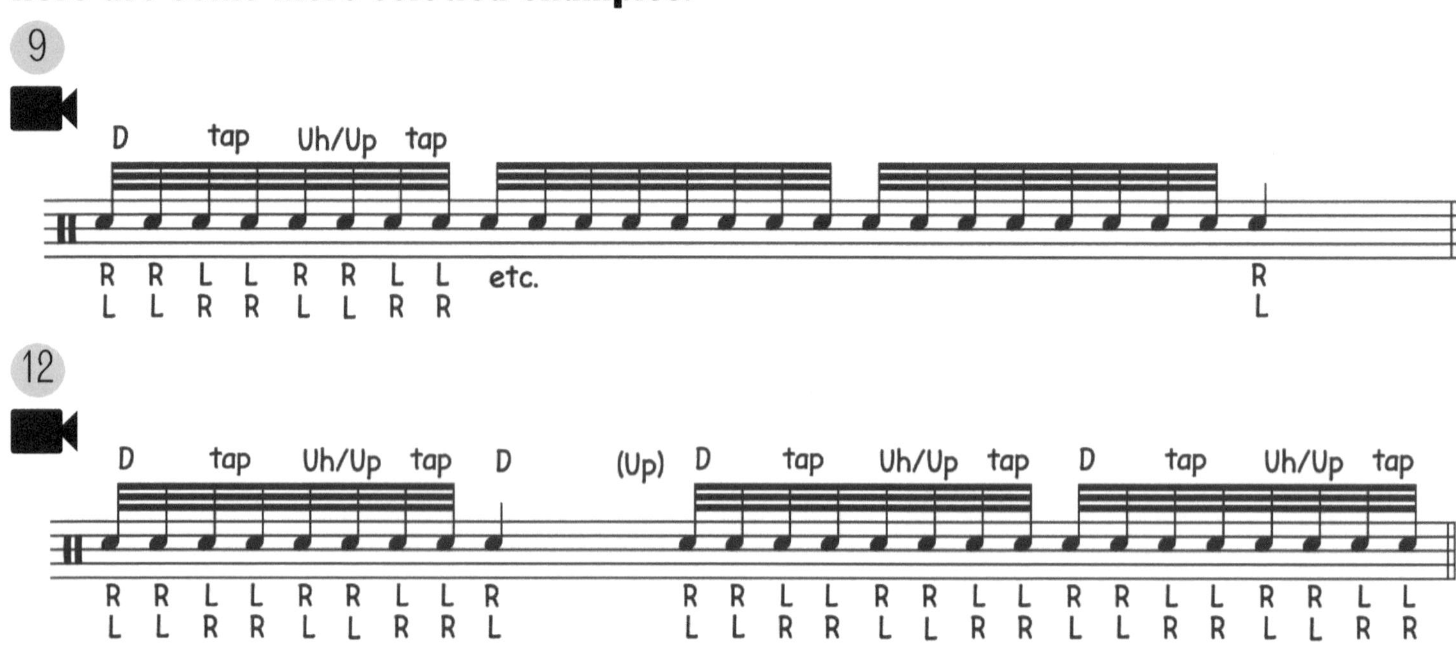

Bruce and Freddie Gruber

20 Bar exercise on page 21:

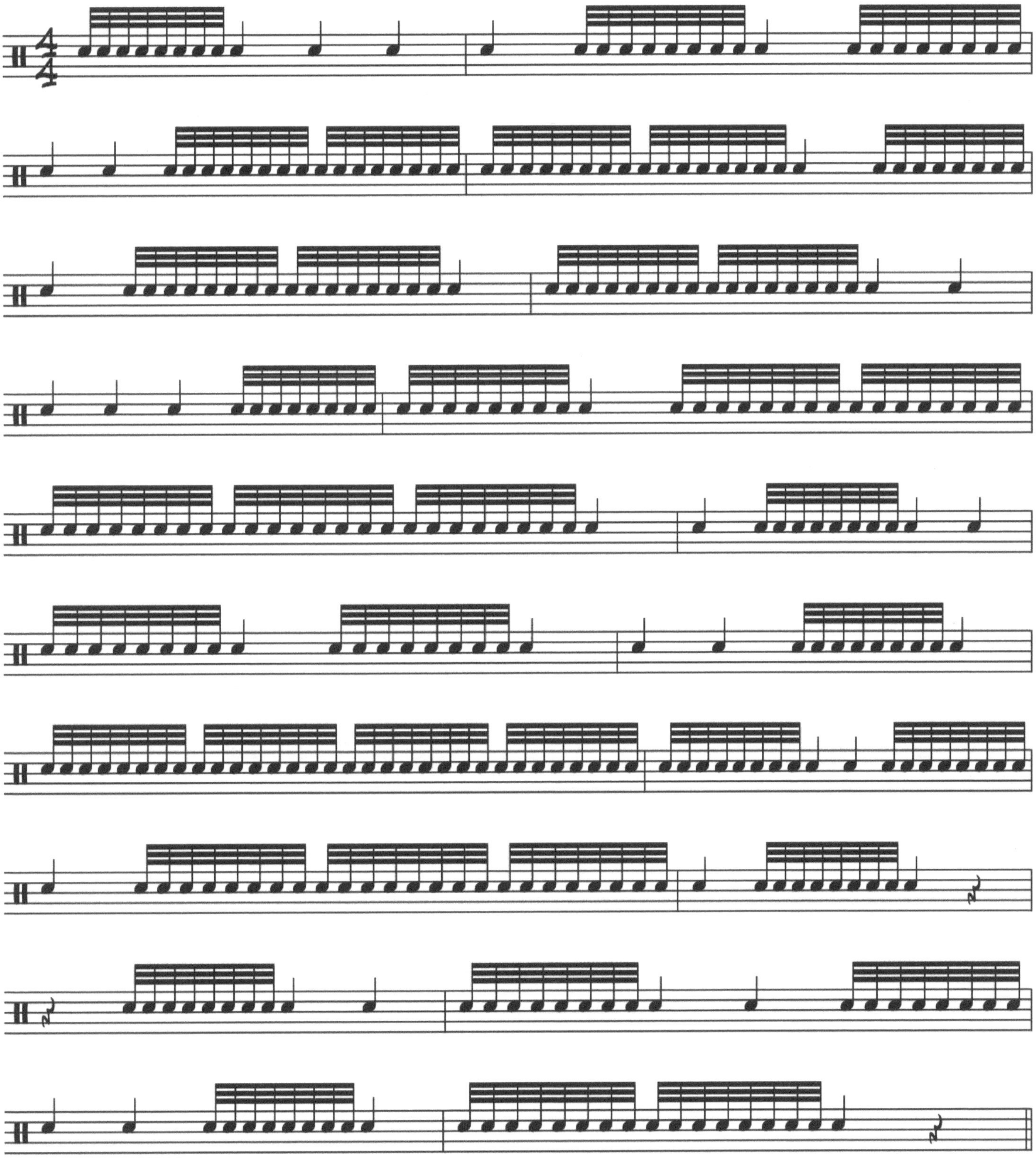

To LH lead

Combining 16th note based rolls with 8th notes

Like pages 16 & 17 use the the same motion. Be sure to orchestrate an easy fluid lift, down and tap. Here are some examples from pages 22 & 23.

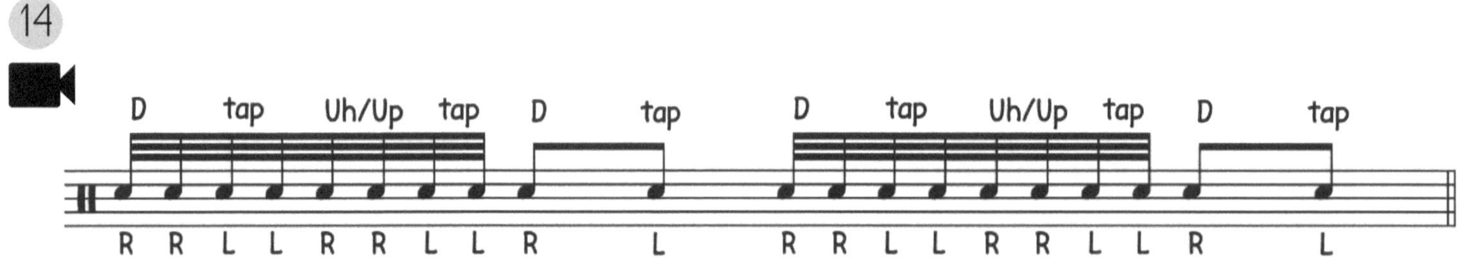

Once these moves become fluid and your dynamics and control are feeling good then continue to the 20 Bar exercise on page 23. Stay firm with a RH lead all the way through the last bar. Then repeat to the LH lead. Stay slow and flow!

20 Bar exercise on page 23:

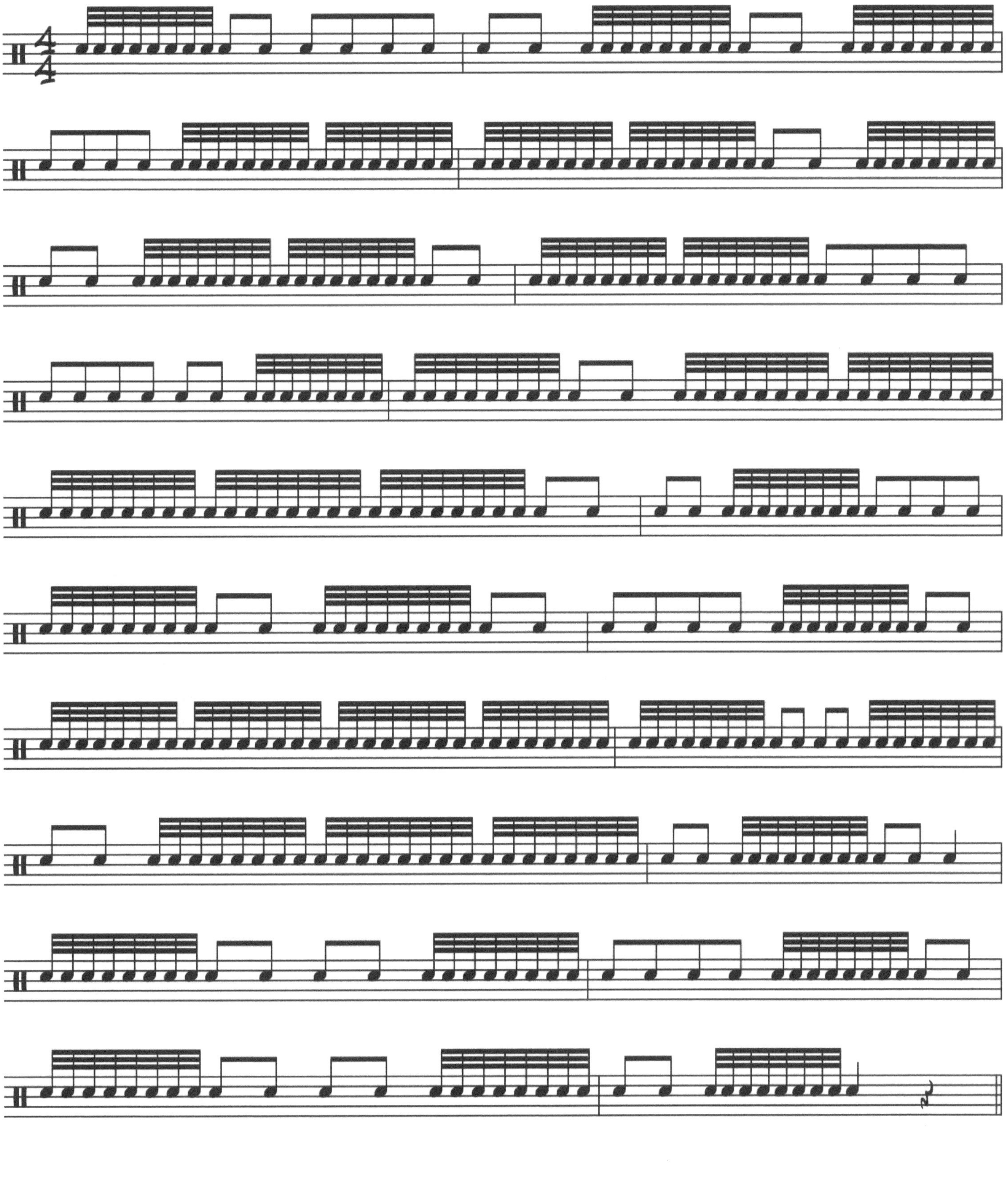

Developing the motion for 5 stroke rolls

Using pages 24 & 25 will give you the opportunity to finetune the delivery system of the 2 variations of the 5 stroke roll. On #1 the motion will go as follows:

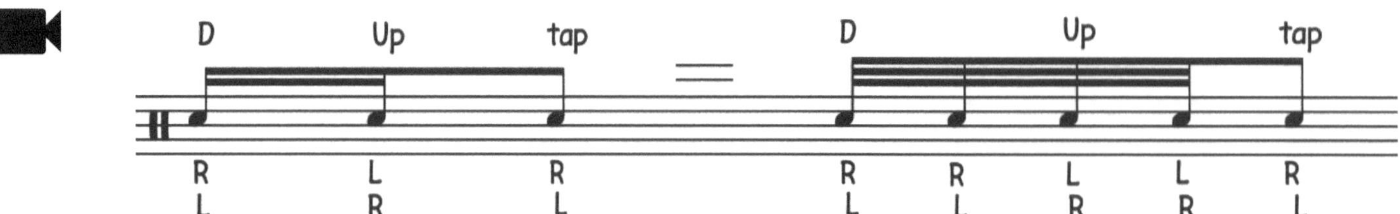

Conceptually you want to come down on the numbers.

Here's Page 24 #1:

1

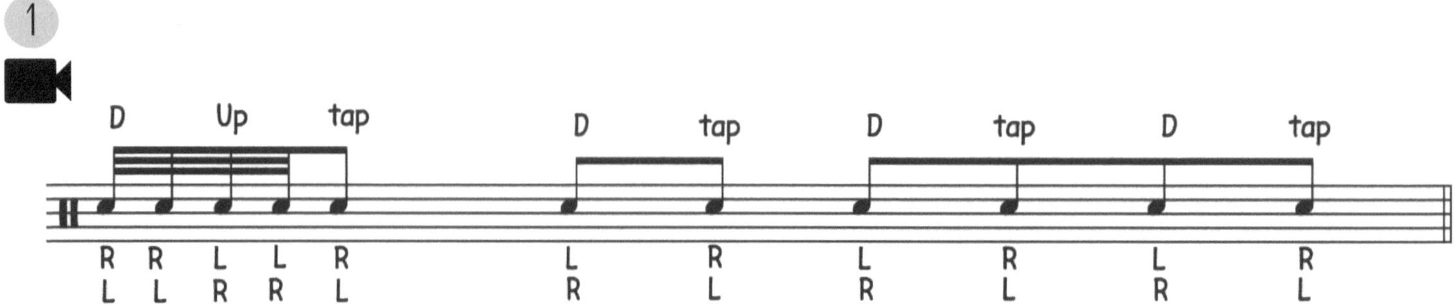

On #2 the orchestration would be more of the traditional 5 stroke roll. While the directive is the same, the rhythm gives it a different flow than the previous demonstration.

Here's Page 24 # 2:

2

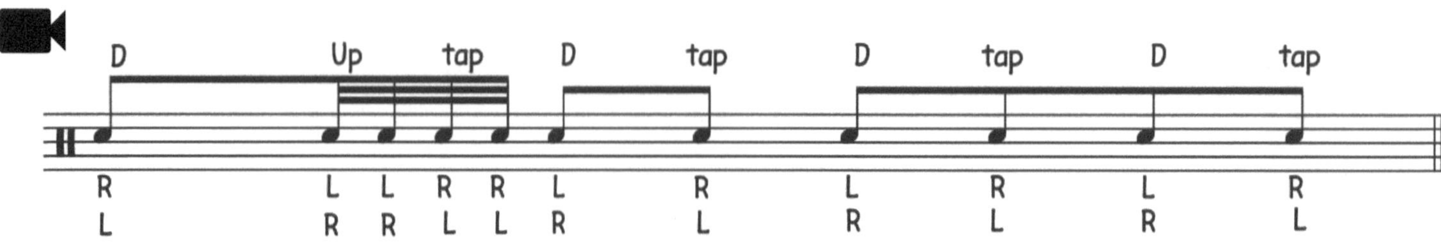

Stay steadfast to the slow open roll and feel the elasticity to the Up strokes. Allow your control of the dynamics start to step forward.

On pages 26-29 you have some nice, flowing extended rolls. When connecting the rolls on these pages adhere to the Down stroke on the numbers concept. There are other ways to orchestrate these rolls, but I am throwing in the good fundamental building blocks for the development of the "inner logic" of movement. Here are some examples:

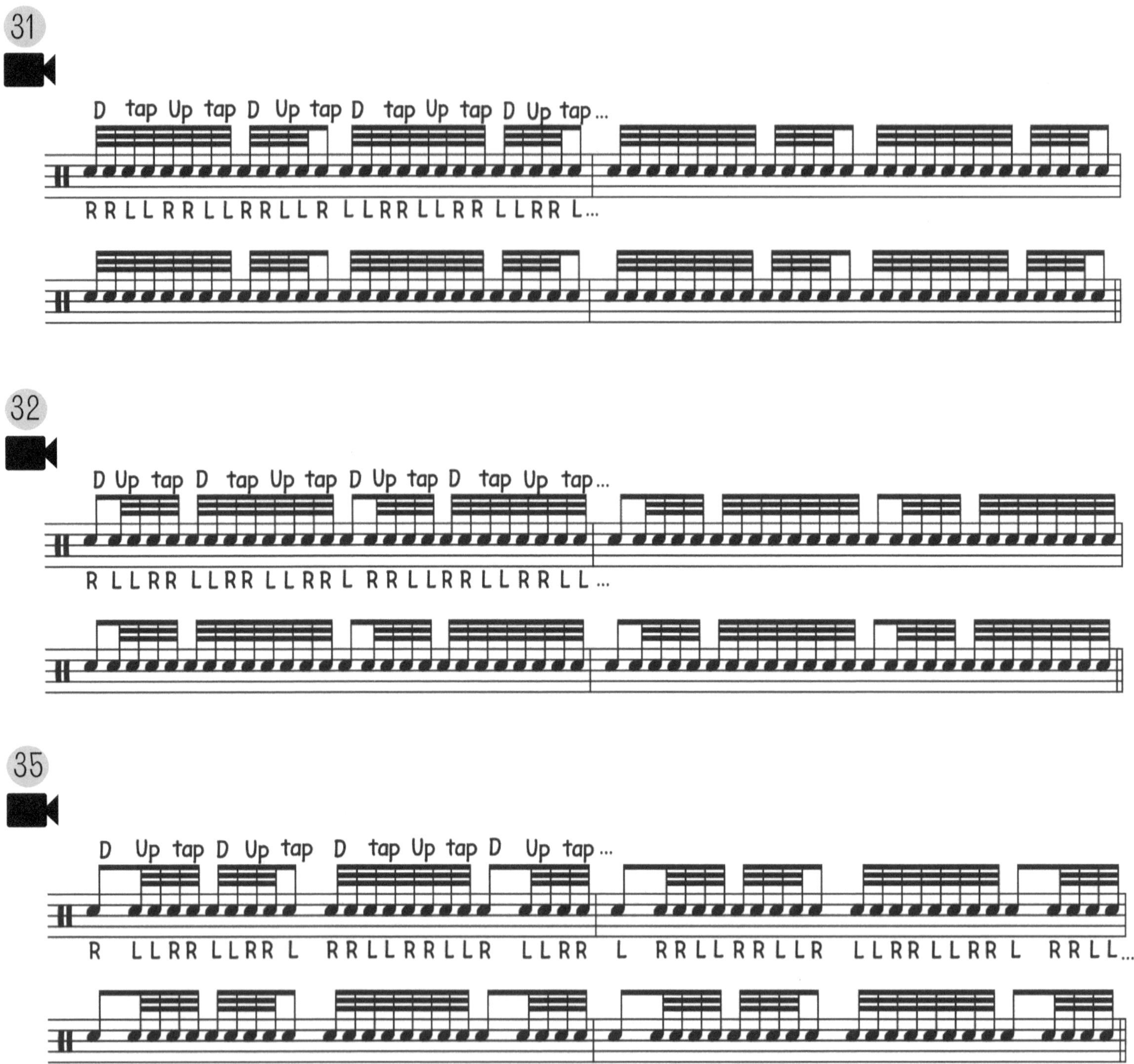

Use these newly acquired movements into Pages 28 & 29. Watch your movement. Stay slow and move eloquently with a spirit of dance. Your rolls should have more elasticity and feel more round.

SECTION 2: Jazz Concepts

In this section, the main concept to begin with is the independence of the motion of the Ride Cymbal pattern. This attention to the flow of the movement will give a deeper development of independence. The motion and flow of the cymbal pattern is the start. There are certainly other aspects to the Ride Cymbal phrasing and delivery of the pattern that would fall into what I call posture and gesture or dialectical nuance. These are more indicative of various musical contributions and should be studied and developed. Once the flow of the Ride Cymbal is feeling consistent then I would like to offer some ideas and concepts for developing Jazz independence, building more conversation skills, and manifesting independence of Left Hand, Right Foot, and Left Foot.

Jazz Ride - Set Up

Breakdown of the Ride Cymbal Movement:

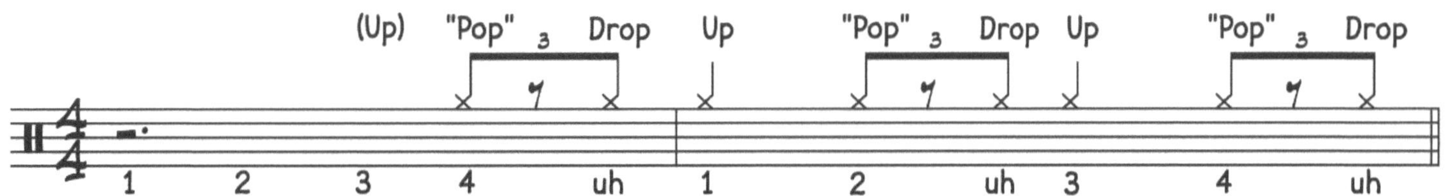

First establish time with the feet. Play the BD on 1-2-3-4 HH on 2 & 4. Feel the support of the flow of the feet. I always say the “conveyor belt of time”! Now enter with the cymbal pattern watching the directive. Allow the Left Hand to play the melody. Get a nice touch and make the phrases have a singsongyness. I made that word up....

Concept 1: Jazz Ride - Snare Melody

Here are some Examples from Pages 34 - 37:

Note: For all the following examples, BD should be played on 1-2-3-4 and HH should be played on 2 & 4.

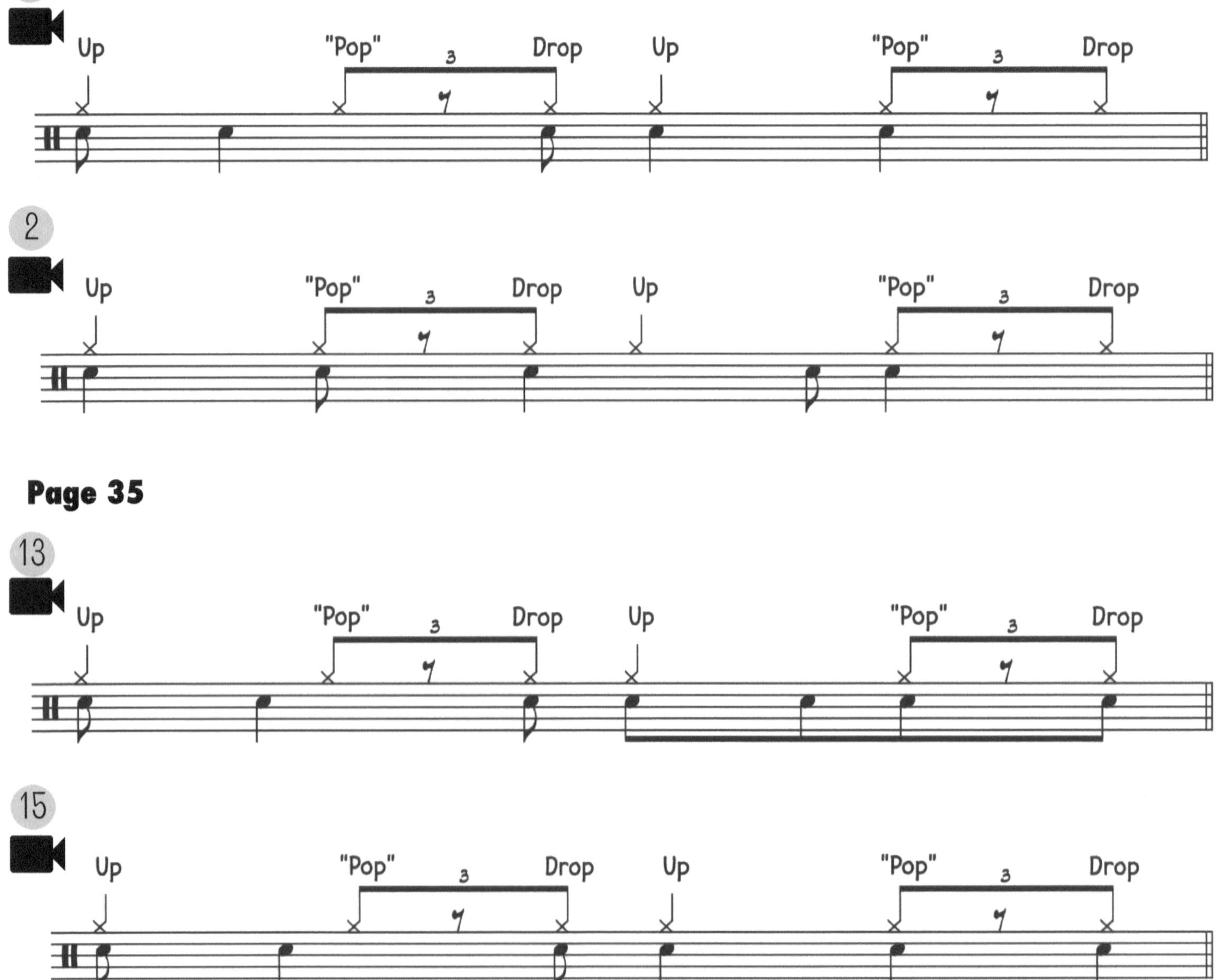

Carry on to Pages 38-45 once the initial 4 bar phrases are comfortable and you feel an essence of dance.

Concept 2: Jazz Ride - Split Melody

Snare on (1 an) and (3 an) BD on (2 an) and (4 an)

Work on an easy conversational approach to the dialogue between Snare and BD. Always put the fluidity of the Ride cymbal beat to the forefront of your attention. Here are some Examples:

Note: For all the following examples, HH should be played on 2 & 4.

Page 34

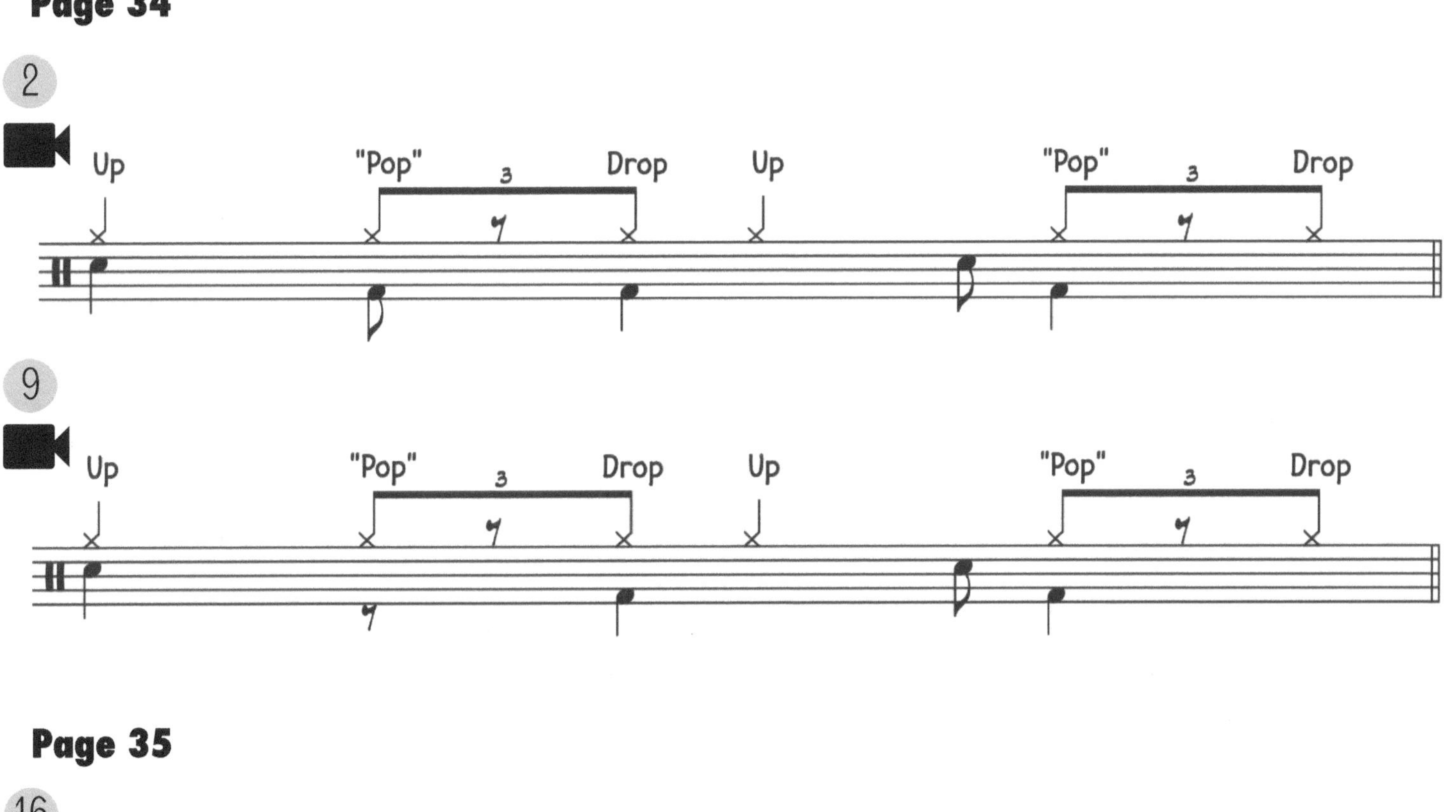

Page 35

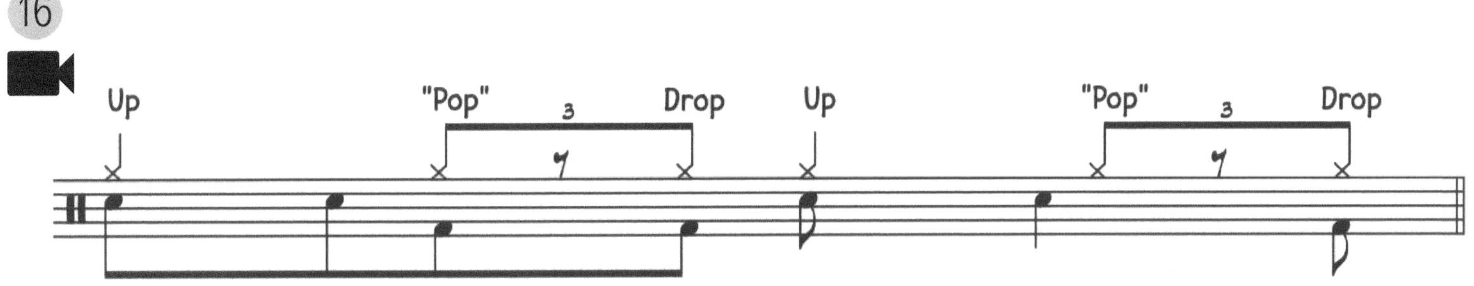

Concept 3: Jazz B - BD Melody

In my daily teaching I use many reference points to label certain exercises. Two of these references would be what I refer to as Jazz A and Jazz B. Jazz B is an ostinato or repetitive phrase, Snare drum playing the 2nd and 3rd partials of the 8th note triplets, while the BD plays the melody. This really establishes a challenge of alignment and calls upon greater sense of independence. Stay with the protocol of movement that you have established with the Ride Cymbal. Equanimity is the key here. Here is the layout of Jazz B and some examples of Jazz B-with BD Melody.

Example of Jazz B

Note: For all the following examples, HH should be played on 2 & 4.

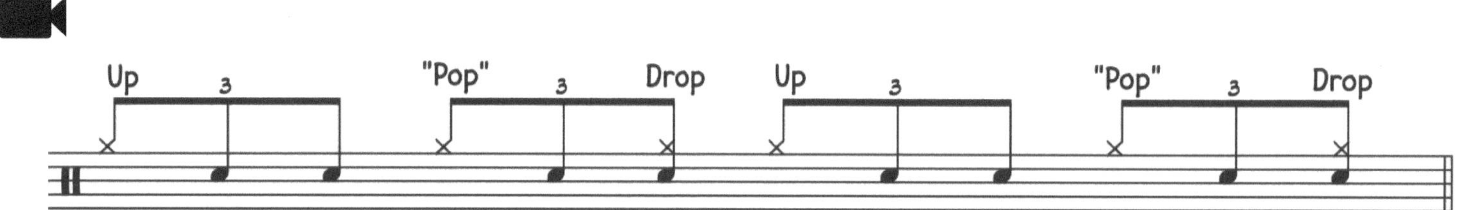

Page 34

1

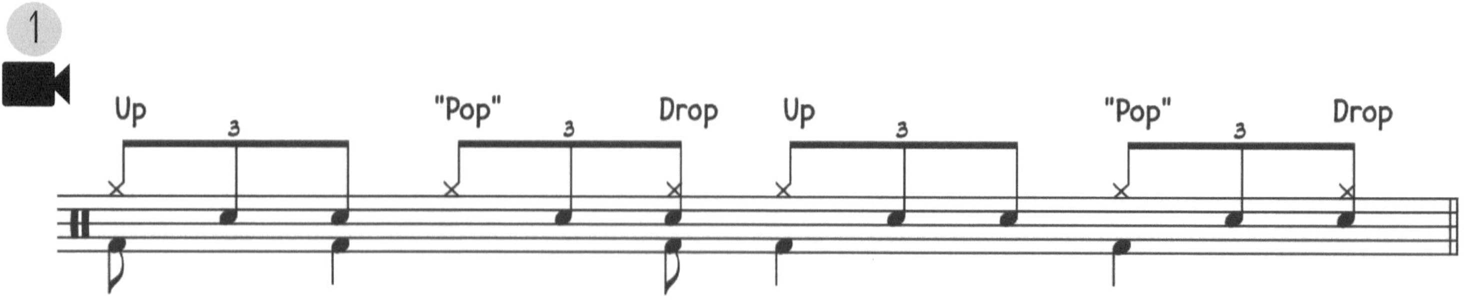

2

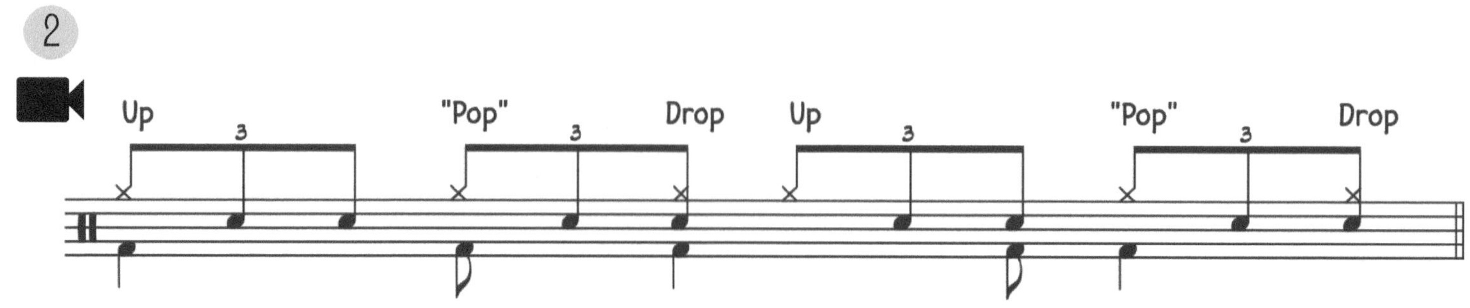

Page 35

13

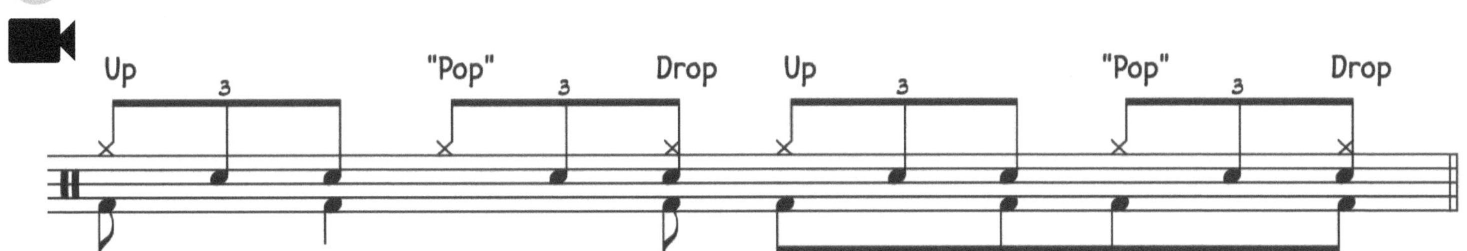

15

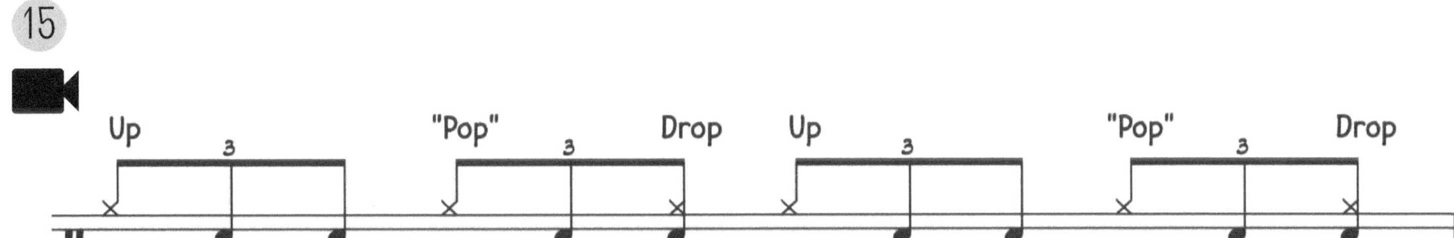

Bruce Masterclass

Bruce and Steve Smith

Concept 4: Jazz B - Alternating Feet

This next concept is an extension to the previous exercises. Now the BD and HH will alternate underneath the Jazz B phrase. Start with R Foot and alternate with L Foot. If there is an even number of notes in the bar then you will return to BD at the start of each bar. When it's and odd number of notes in the bar then you will start with BD on the 1st bar then HH on the 2nd bar etc. This really helps to develop a keen sense of balance as the 2 feet work together to play the rhythmic phrases under the Jazz B. Stay slow and feel the control and articulation while maintaining fluidity with the Ride cymbal pattern. Super challenging!

Here are a few examples:

Page 34

1

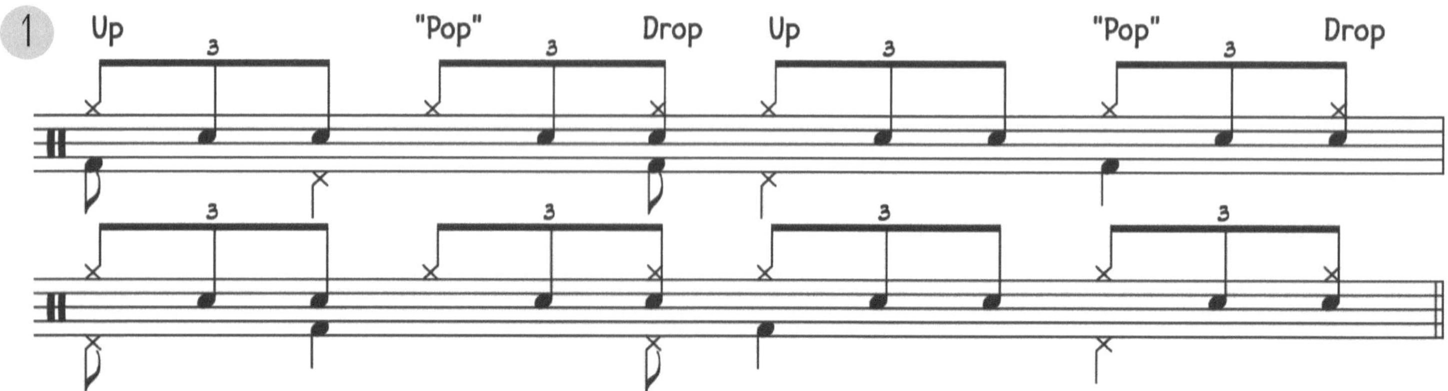

5

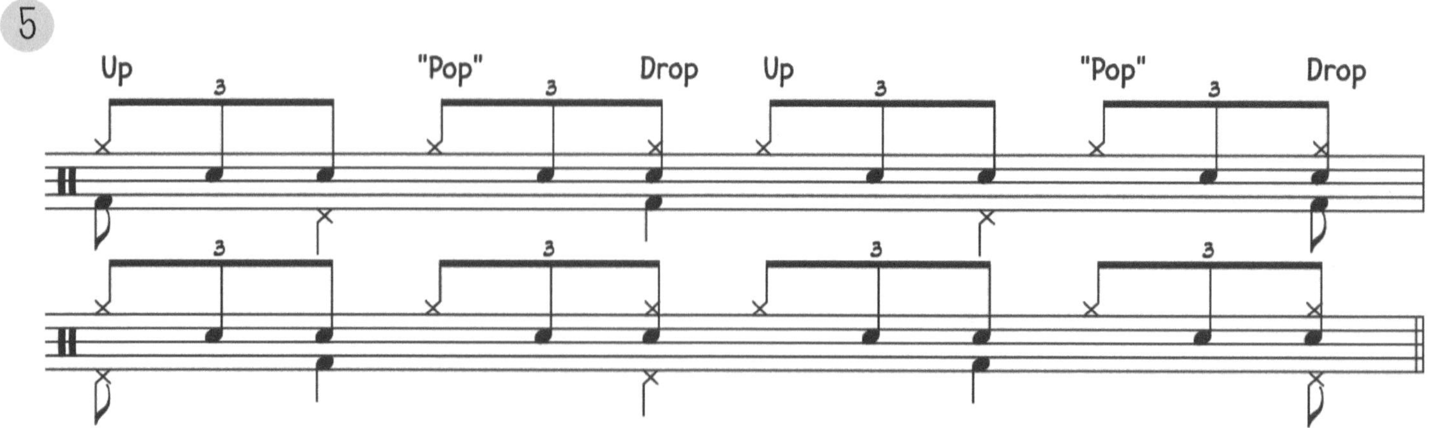

Page 35

18

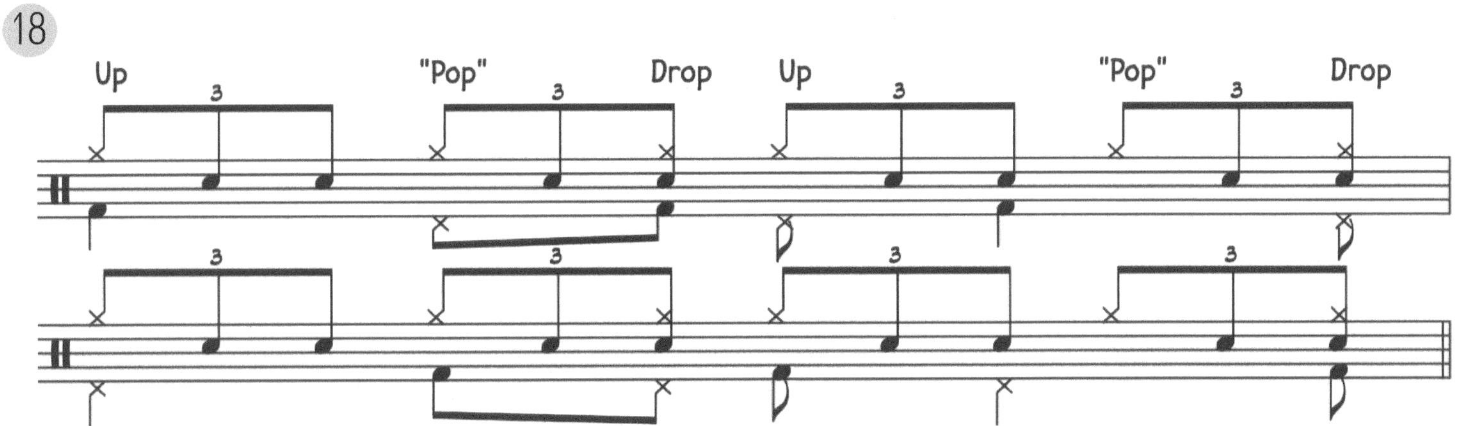

22

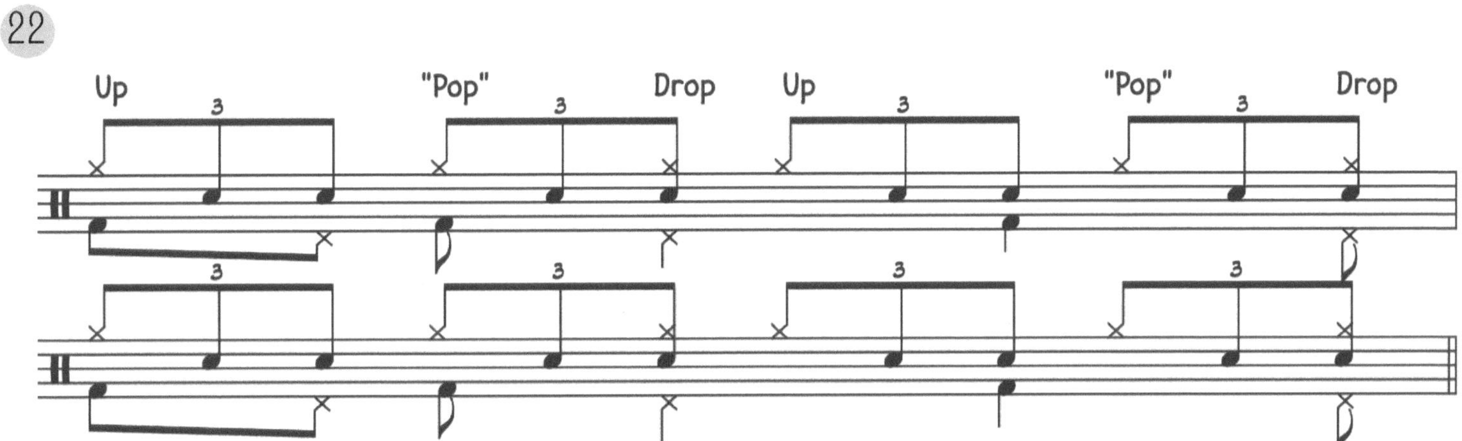

Bruce with Dave Atkinson, Gregg Bissonette, Benny Greb, and Jared Falk (Left to Right)

Concept 5: The "Elvin"

This next series of exercises were designed to capture some of the essence of Elvin Jones. His contributions and unique approach are a large branch on the tree of drums. In my pursuit of accessing some of the flow and freedom that I was seeking from being inspired by Elvin, I came up with this approach. The rules for the following have some potential alternative options, however I have my specific directions. You are to fill in the space around the BD melody with the snare drum. Rule #1...Don't play more than 2 triplets in a row with the LH Snare. This means some of these need to drop a triplet out. Rule #2... The triplet phrase of choice where applicable is "an uh". Some of these exercise will work out without any adjustments.

Here are some of the Examples:

Page 34

1

On this particular phrase you will not play beat 1 of the triplet partial.

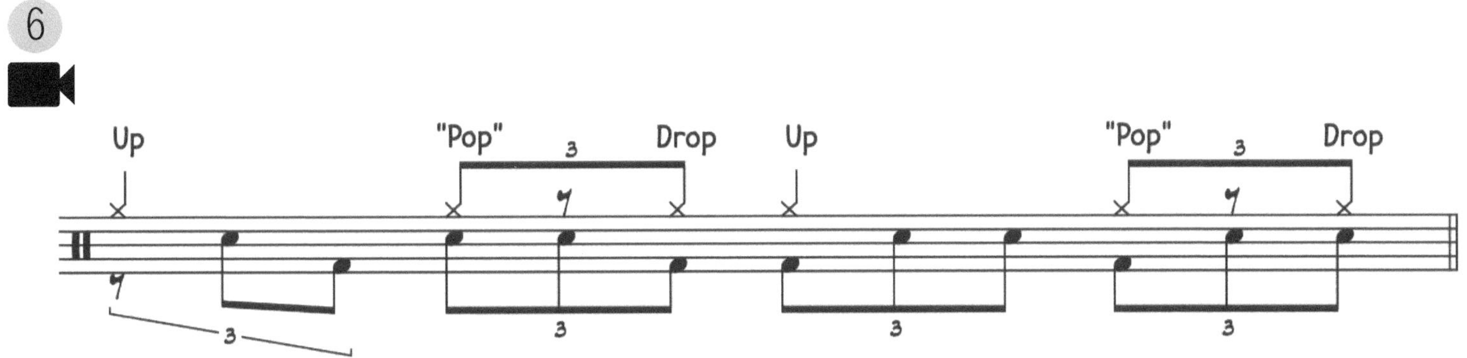

On this particular phrase you will not play many of the triplet partials.

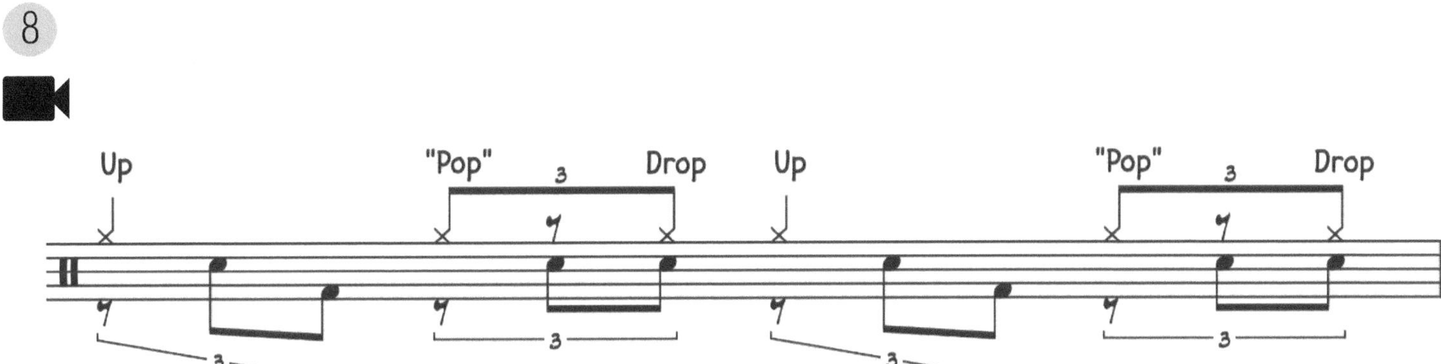

Bruce and Dom Famularo

Concept 6: The "Elvin" With Drags

Continuing the Theme from the previous exercises, you can put Drags on some the phrases where there is only a middle note of the triplet to be played. There is a dialectical nuance that can be added to flavor the phrasing of Drags.

Here are some of those examples:

Page 34

1

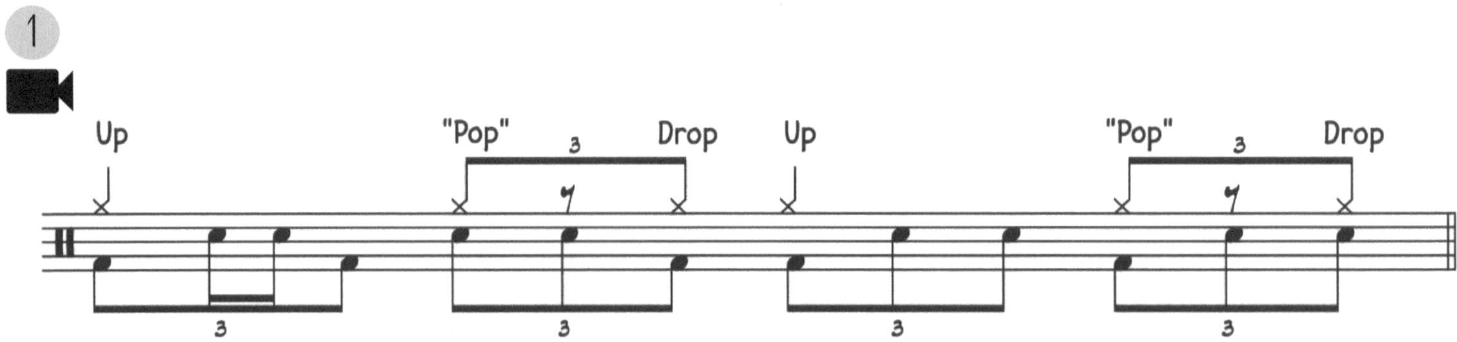

2

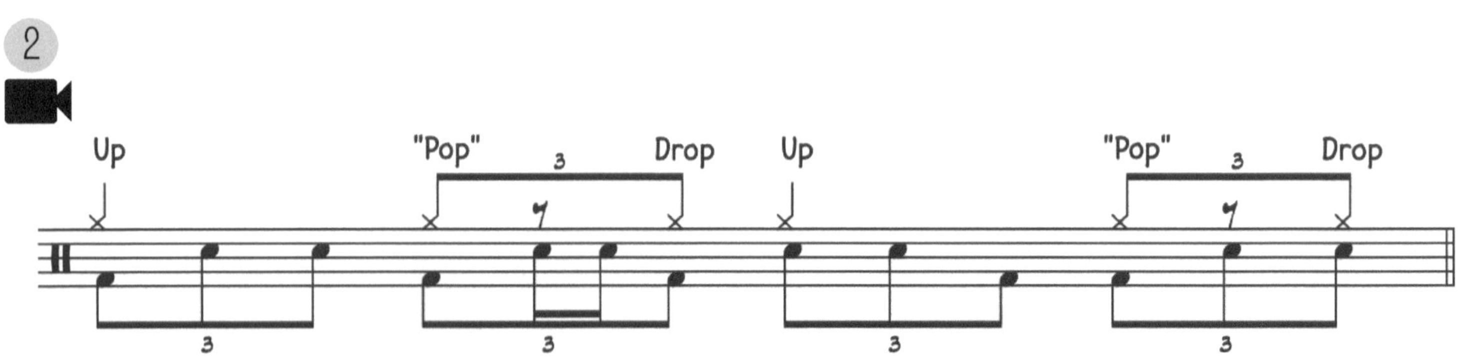

Concept 7: The "Elvin" With 16ths

The following concept puts another challenge to the stability and integrity of the triplet based rhythm used for the Ride Cymbal Pattern by adding 16th notes as your Left Hand rhythm, while maintaining a Triplet Feel with the Right Hand. These exercises can also be adjusted to having the ride cymbal rhythm be played as a dotted 8th 16th version.

Here are some examples:

Page 34

1

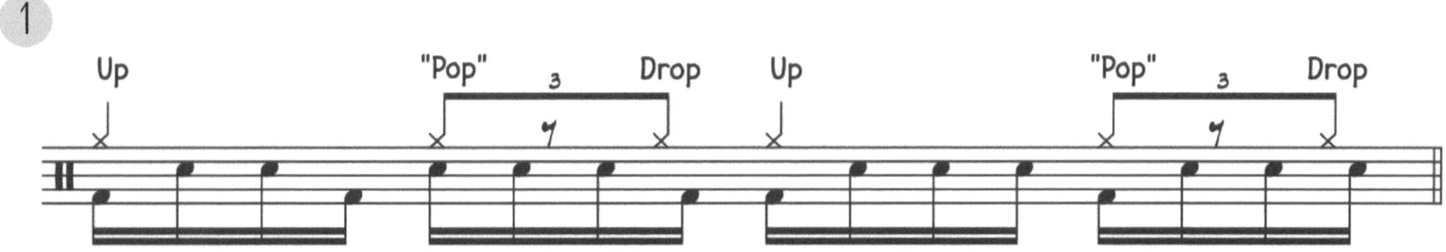

8

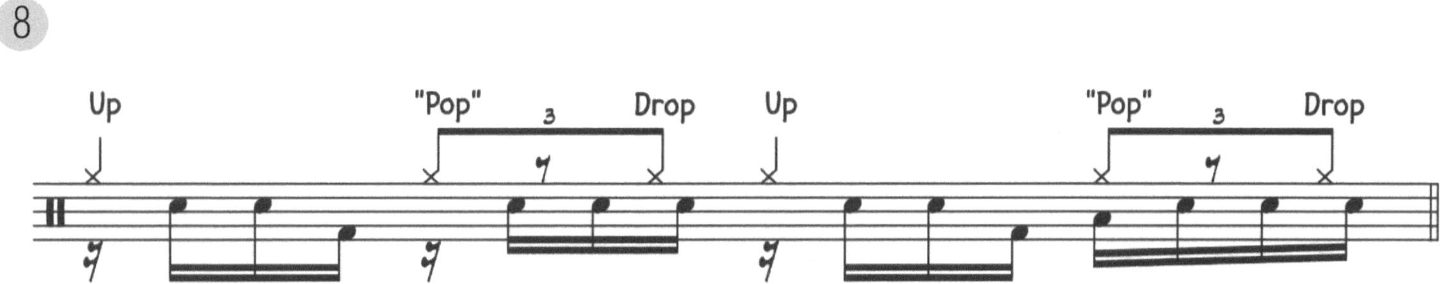

Concept 8: The "Elvin" With Split Feet

The layout for this concept is to split the melody between the HH and BD. Start with the HH playing the (1 an) & (3 an) and the BD playing the (2 an) & (4 an). You can also reverse the order. This concept really adds a challenge to the flow between feet and hands. Keep your attention to the fluidity of the Ride Cymbal pattern maintaining the directive.

Page 34

3

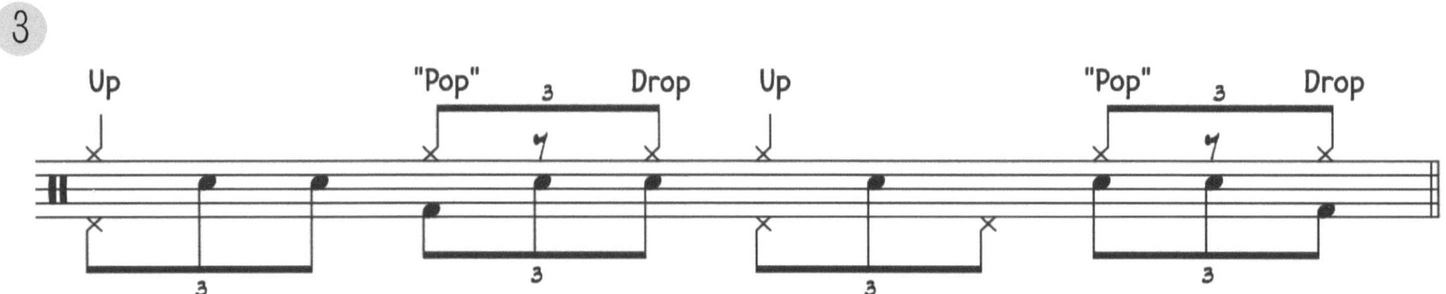

5

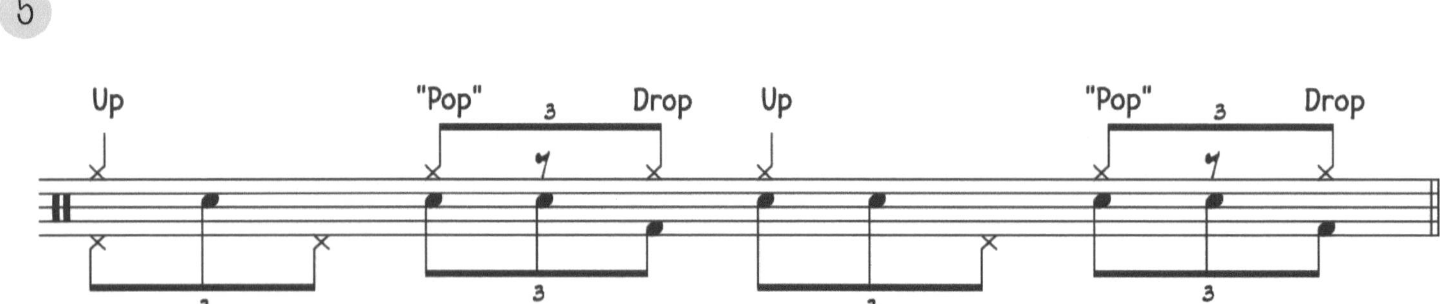

Concept 9: The Dotted Quarter

In this series of exercises the BD will play dotted quarter notes. The repetition of the phrase will reboot every 3 bars. This really opens up some nice contrapuntal phrasing as the BD weaves around the steady melody in the Left Hand. I recommend playing all of Page 34. Then try applying the dotted quarter to the Left Hand and let the BD play the melody.

Page 34

1

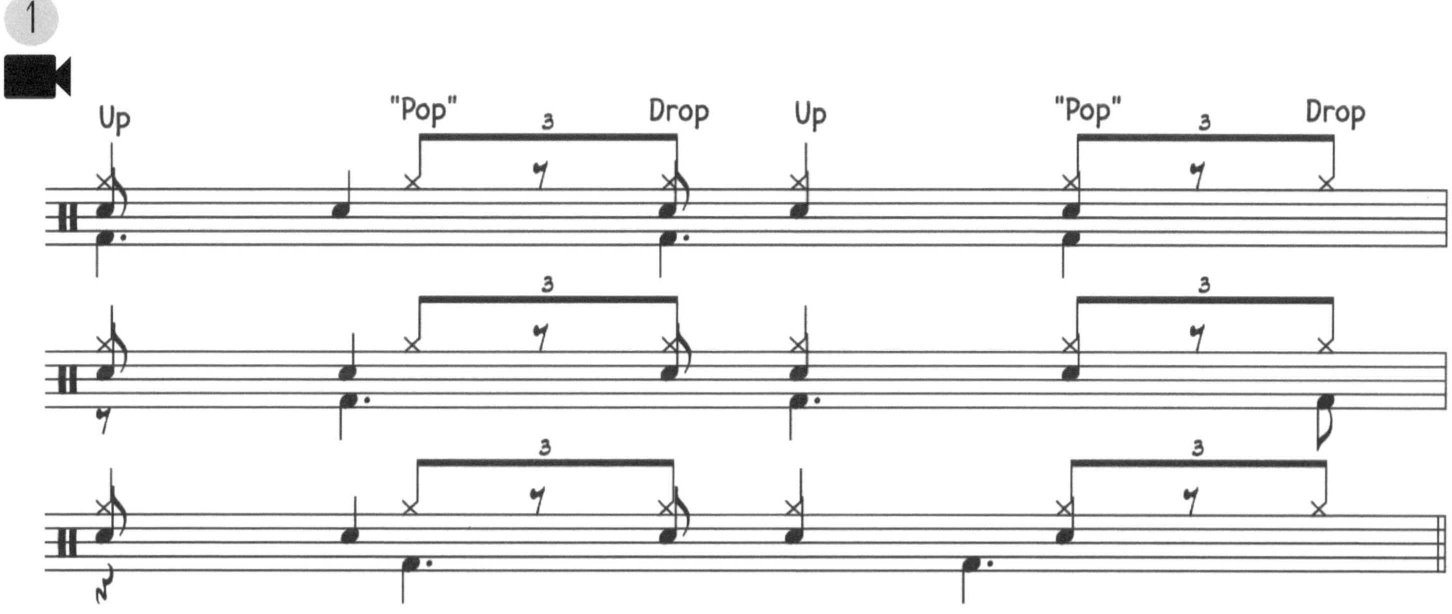

3

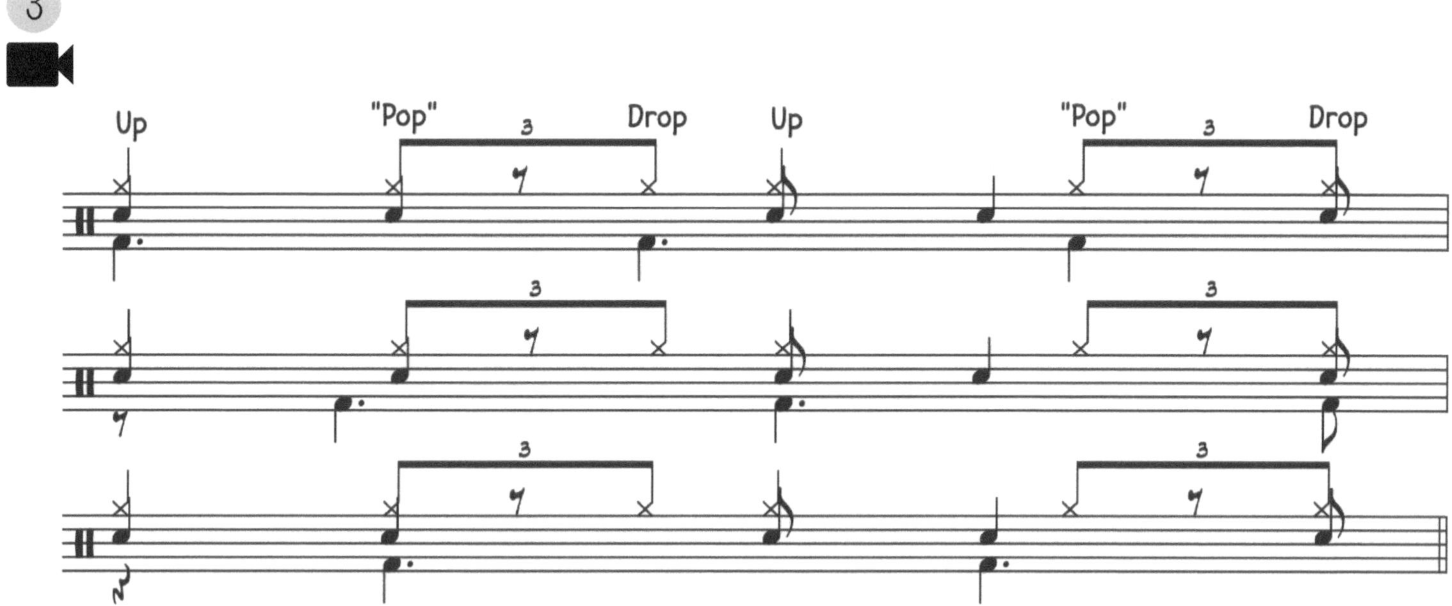

Page 35

14

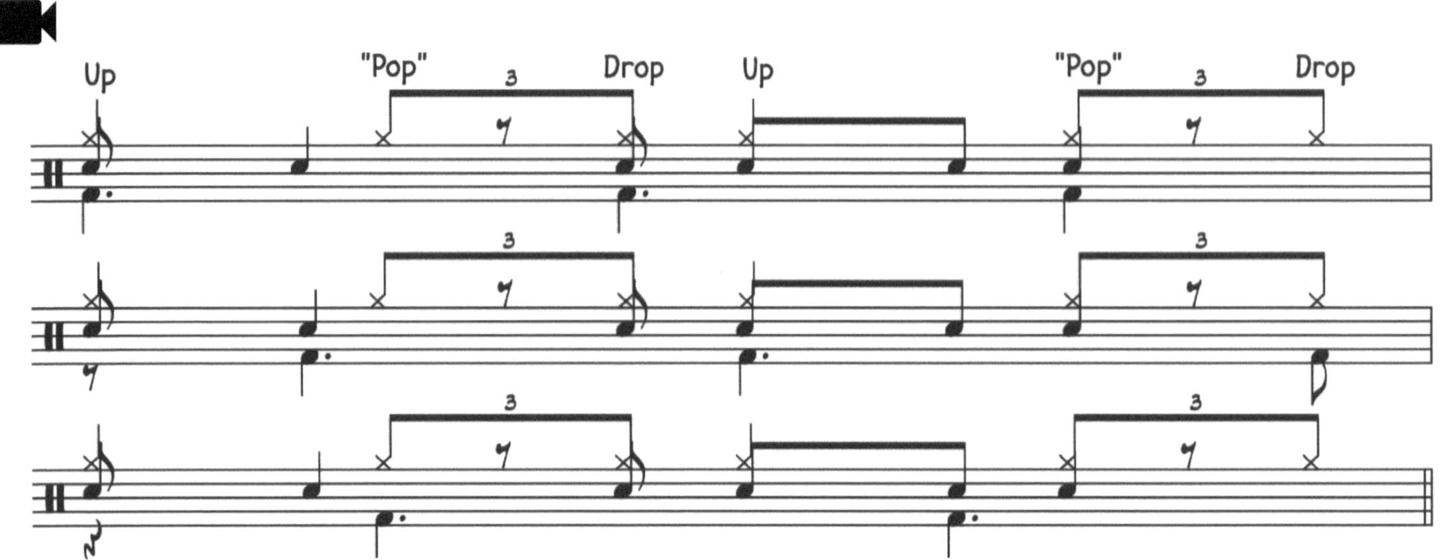

17

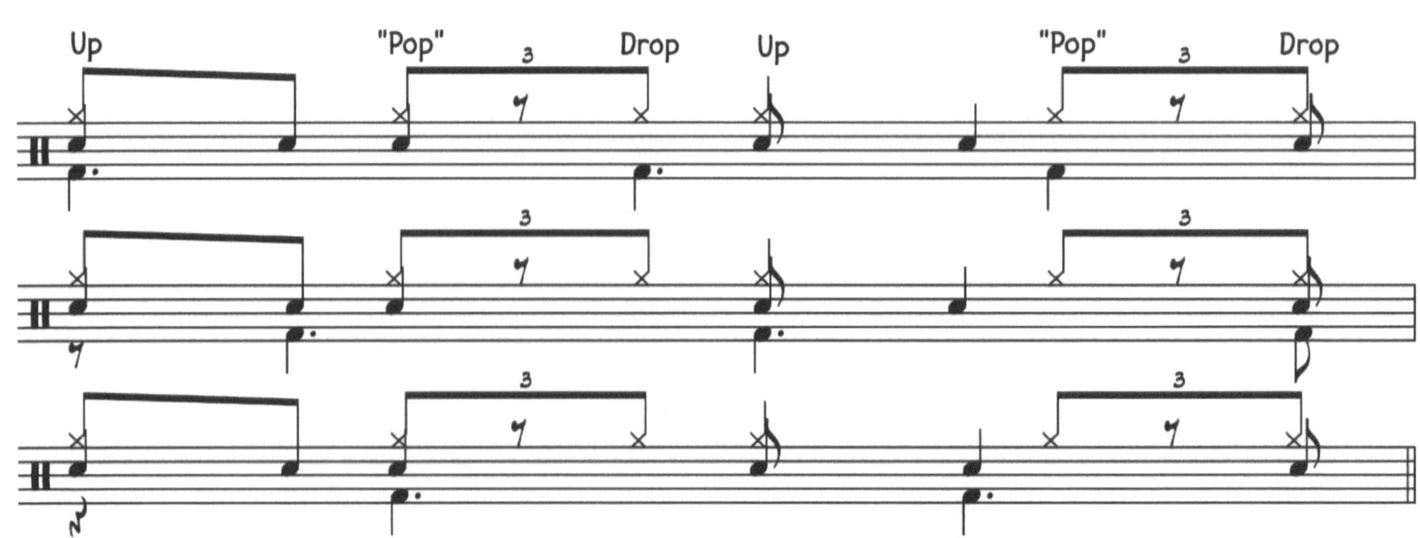

SECTION 3: Simple Rock n Roll Concepts

In this next series of interpretations I use pages 10 & 11 for simplicity of reading while adapting the concept to Rock patterns. The layout is: play BD on "1 an" and "3 an" and Snare drum on "2 an" and "4 an" where applicable.

Page 10

20 Bar exercise on page 11:

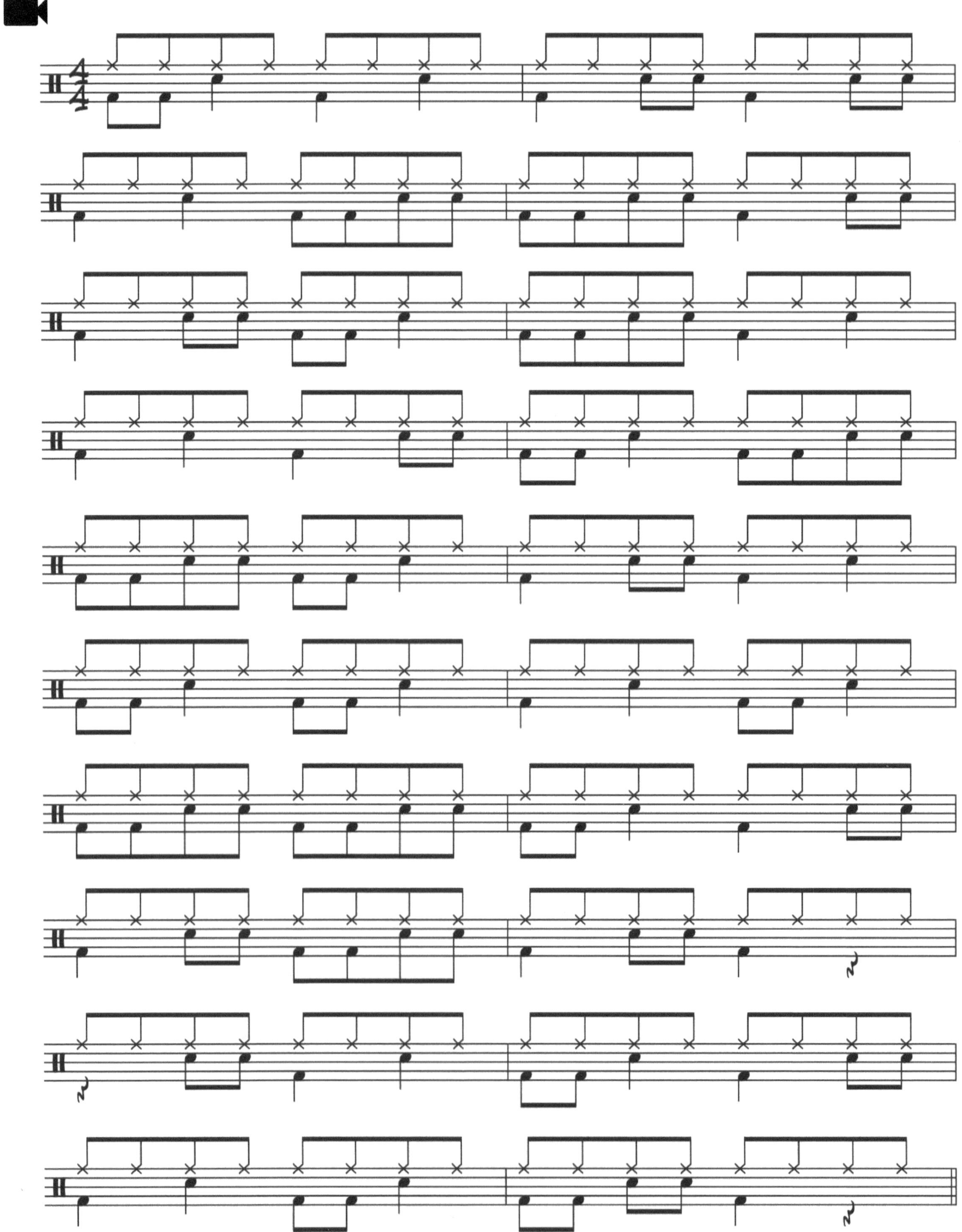

Rock Concepts Continued

The theme continues for Pages 12 & 13 converting these into Rock patterns. The layout is play BD on (1 uh) & (3 uh) and Snare drum on (2 uh) & (4 uh) where applicable.

Page 12

5

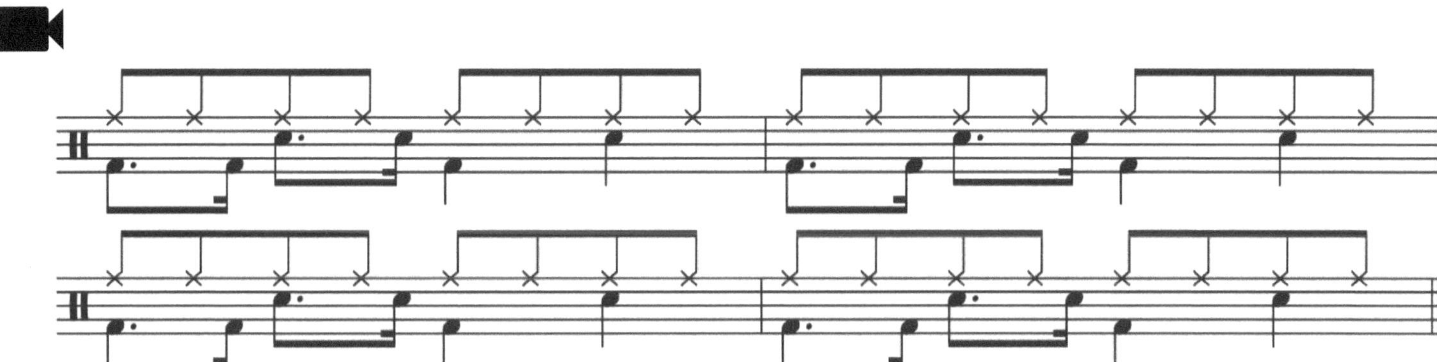

8

Page 13

13

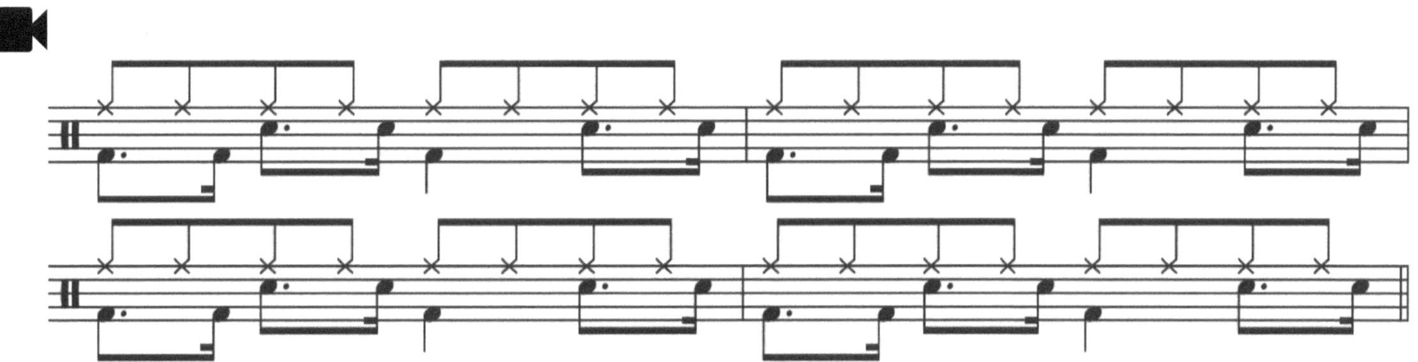

20 Bar exercise on page 13:

SECTION 4: Brazilian Concepts

The Bossa Nova - Snare Drum melody

Using pages 34 - 45, play the Snare drum melody while playing 8th notes on the Cymbal or HH with the Bossa Nova BD pattern. If playing 8th notes on the Cymbal, play HH foot on 2 & 4.

Bossa Pattern:

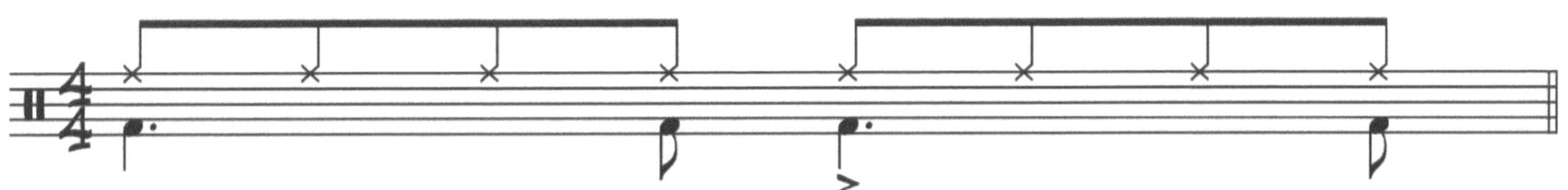

Page 34

7

9

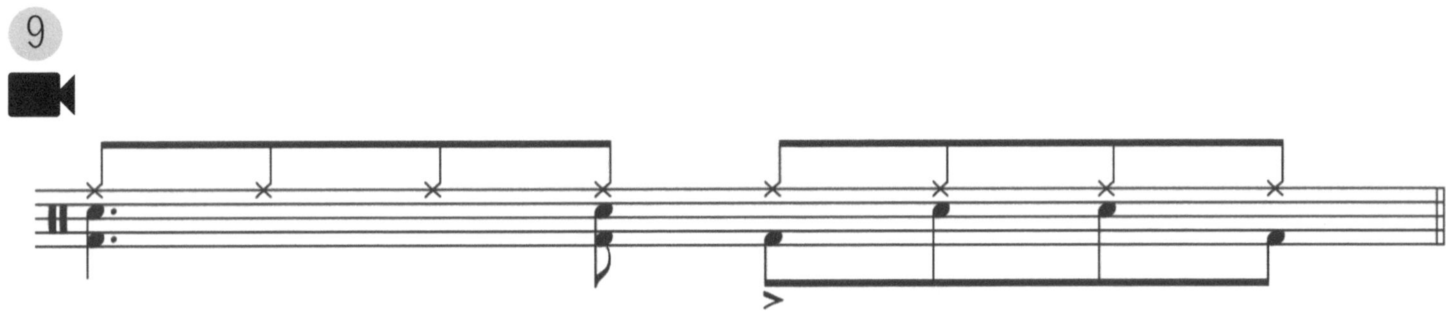

The Bossa Nova - Split The Melody

This version you will play the 8th notes on the Ride cymbal. With the Left hand, split the bar in half and play the (1 an 2 an) on the Floor Tom then the (3 an 4 an) on the Small Tom. This creates a nice melodic twist.

Page 34

1

5

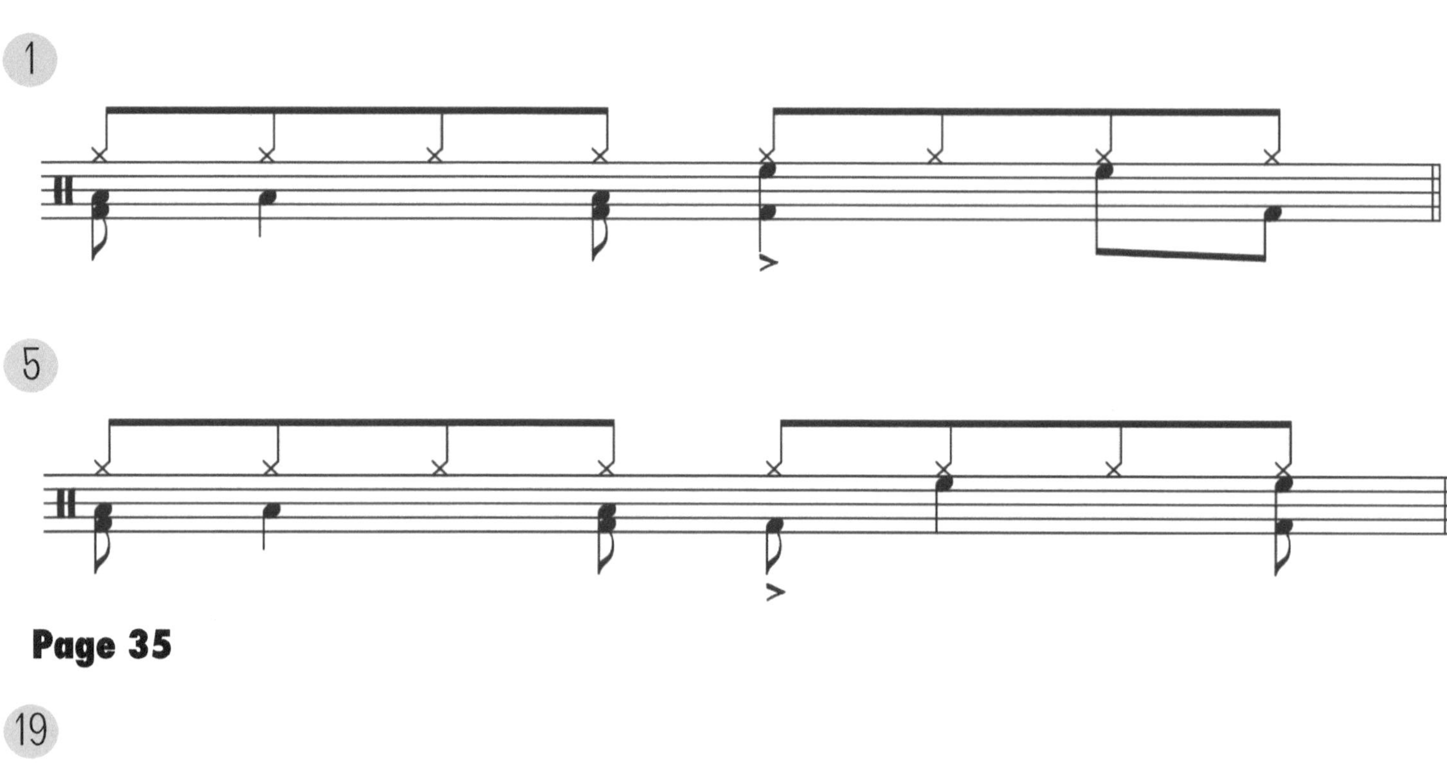

Page 35

19

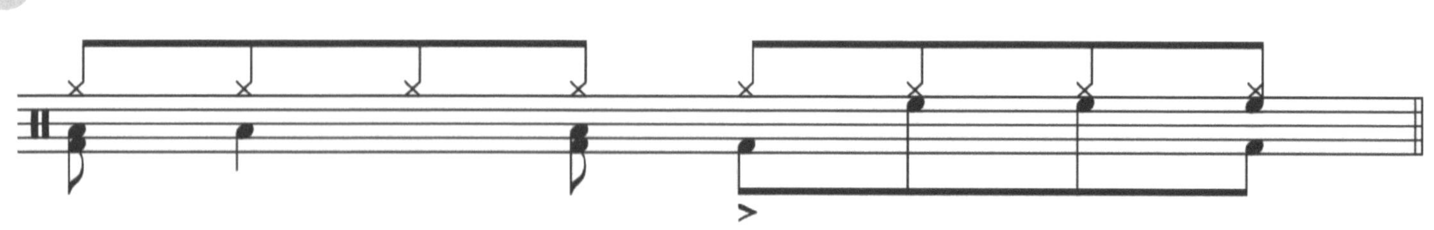

Bruce and Vic Firth

BD Options:

Experiment with using the following BD patterns within the previous exercises.

Option #2:

Experiment with creating four measure phrases using option #2 as the BD pattern for measures 3 and 4.

Page 35

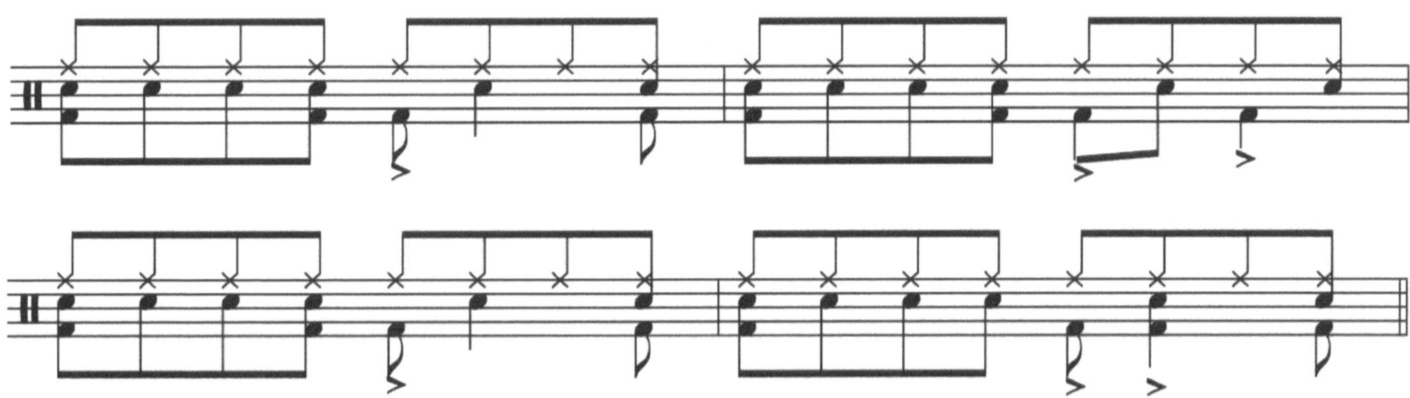

The Broken Cymbal Pattern - Snare Drum Melody

Using the same layout for the Bossa Nova, play the Broken cymbal pattern of (1 2 an 3 4 an) and play the Snare drum as the melody. This should be played at a brisk tempo. While the independence and freedom of playing these rhythms are one goal, find the patterns that speak to you and find your groove.

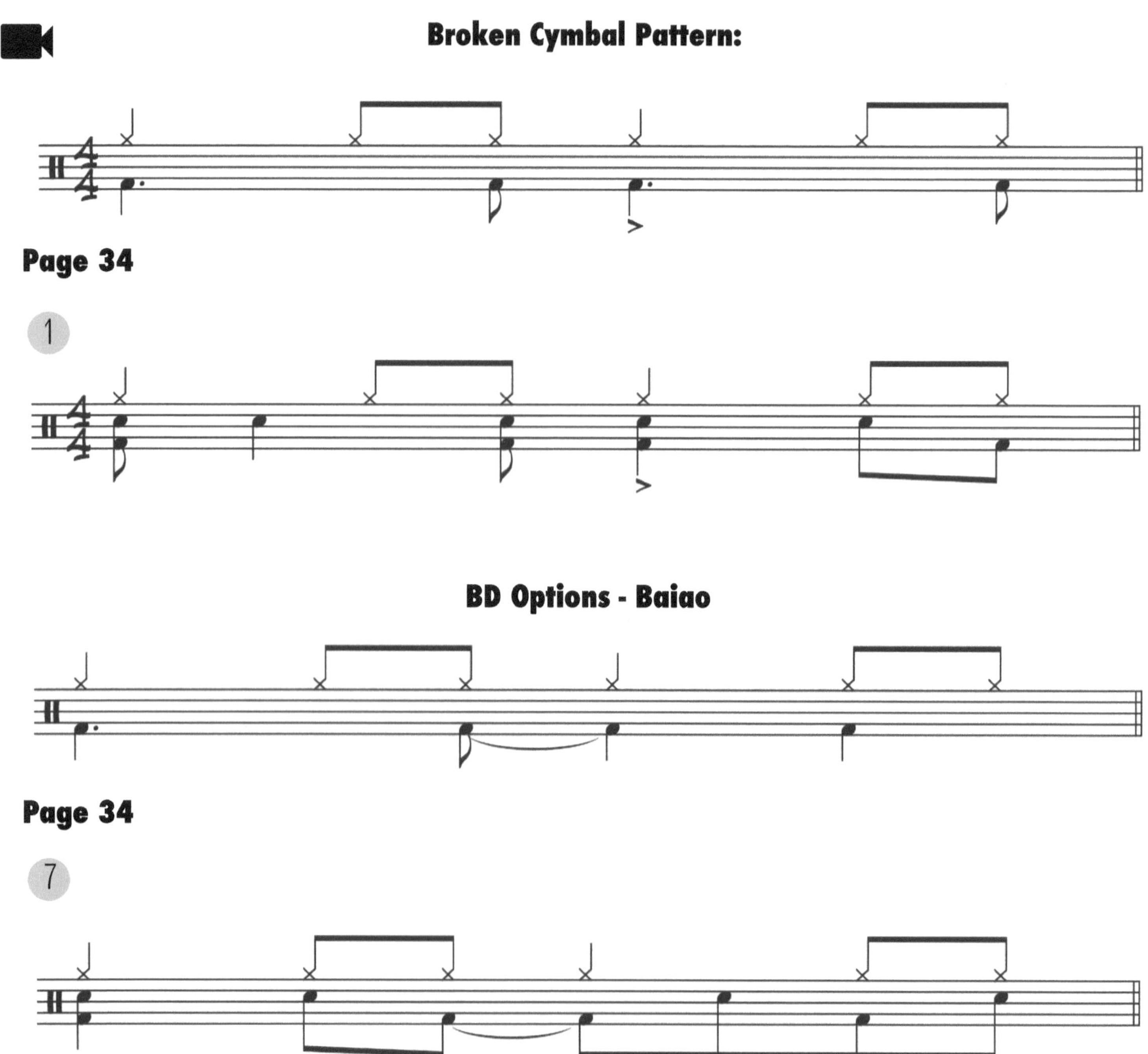

BD Options - Surdo (Option #1)

Page 34

1

BD Options - Option #2 (Four Measure Phrase)

Experiment with creating four measure phrases using option #2 as the BD pattern for measures 3 and 4.

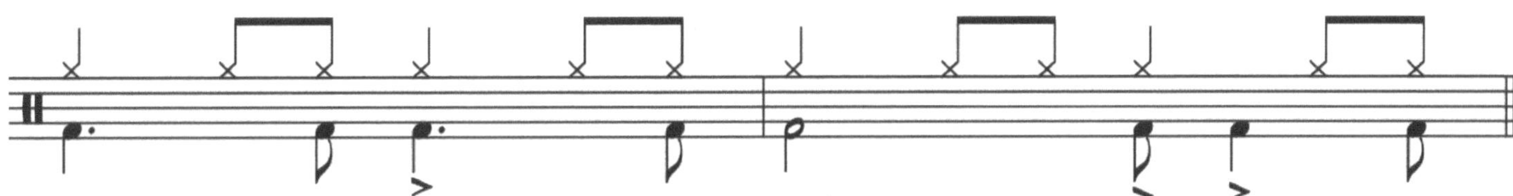

Page 34

1

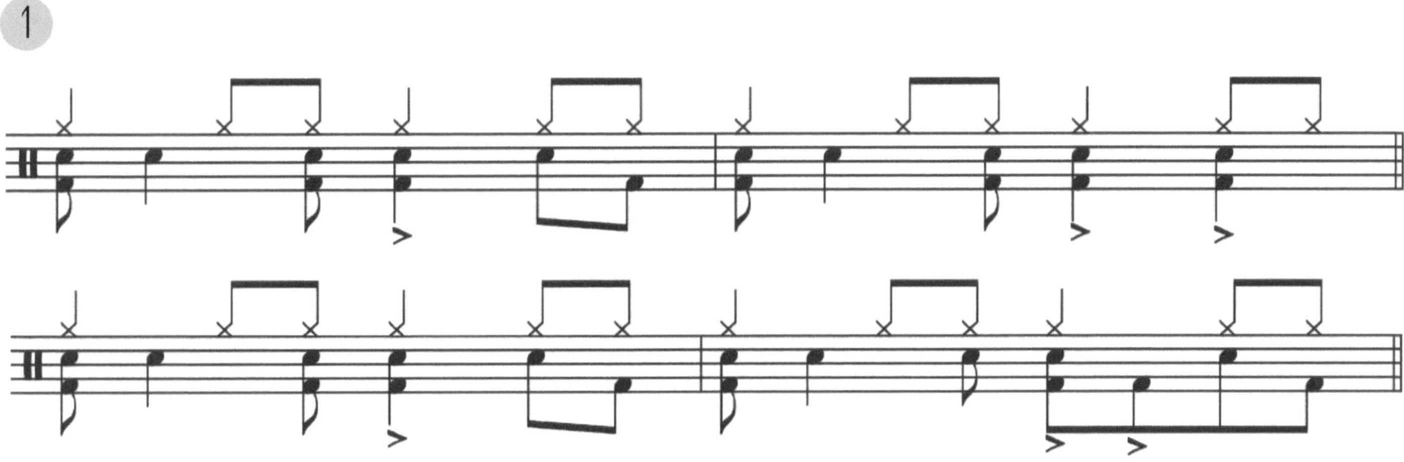

SECTION 5: Choreographing Your Moves

These next exercises are designed to help with your development and freedom of movement around the Kit. The initial set up will use Page 54 #11 and Page 55 #25, 29 & 30. These will be used to set up a basic understanding of orchestration of the moves, to build "the inner logic of movement". Once these are established the next phase will use page 56 (#37 - 44) In pursuance of a slow and fluid orchestration, I use a rhythmic modulation to help induce a deeper insight to enhance greater control and fluidity of your movement. The 2 rhythms are quarter note triplets and 8th note triplets. Execute all triplets in Section 5 with single strokes. By going through this modulation you can track the dance of your moves more effectively!

Page 54

11

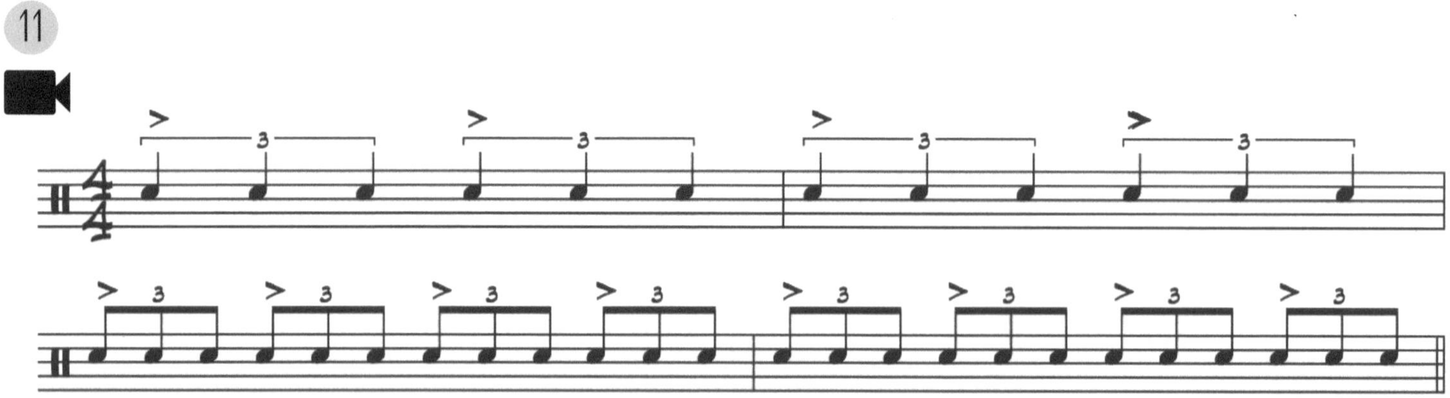

Page 55

25

29

30

Bruce and Carter McLean

A Young Bruce On His Ludwigs

Moving The Accents To Toms

While going through these exercises play close attention to the fluidity of your movement. Feel the arc from the center of the snare drum out to the toms.

Page 56

37

38

41

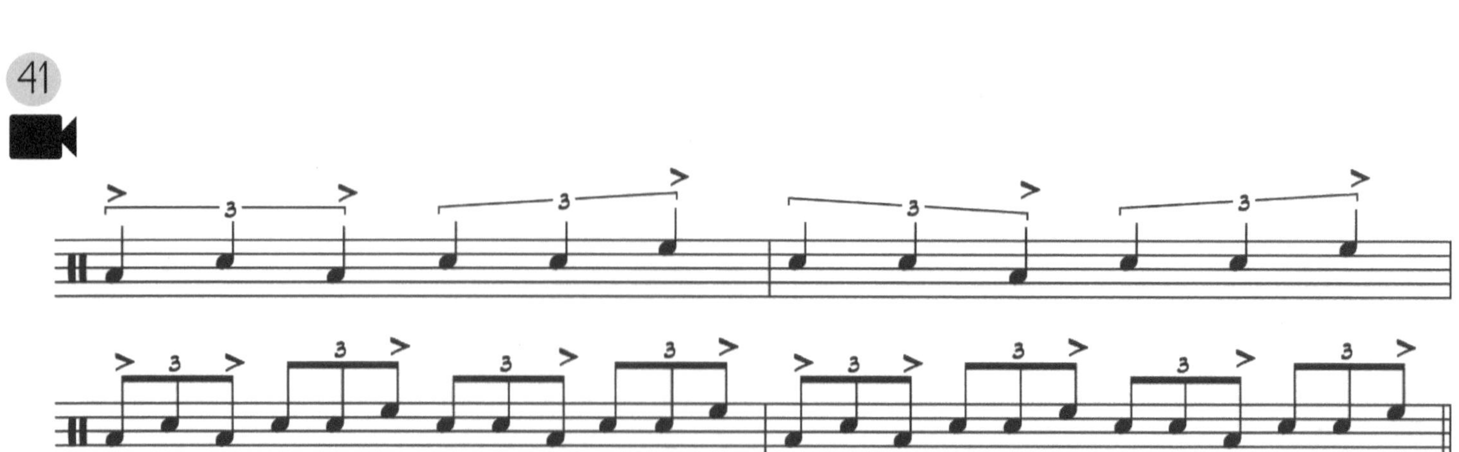

Moving The Accents To Snare

In this next section you will reverse the motion by placing the accents on the snare and the unaccented notes on the Toms territorially. Meaning the RH will play the unaccented notes on the Floor Tom and the LH will play the unaccented notes to the Small Tom. This creates not only a bit of a challenge for the movement but also for the ear to acclimate to the interval of the toms and how they play into the melodic structure of each pattern. Again play the 2 rhythmic phrases as quarter note triplets to 8th note triplets.

Here are some examples:

Page 56

37

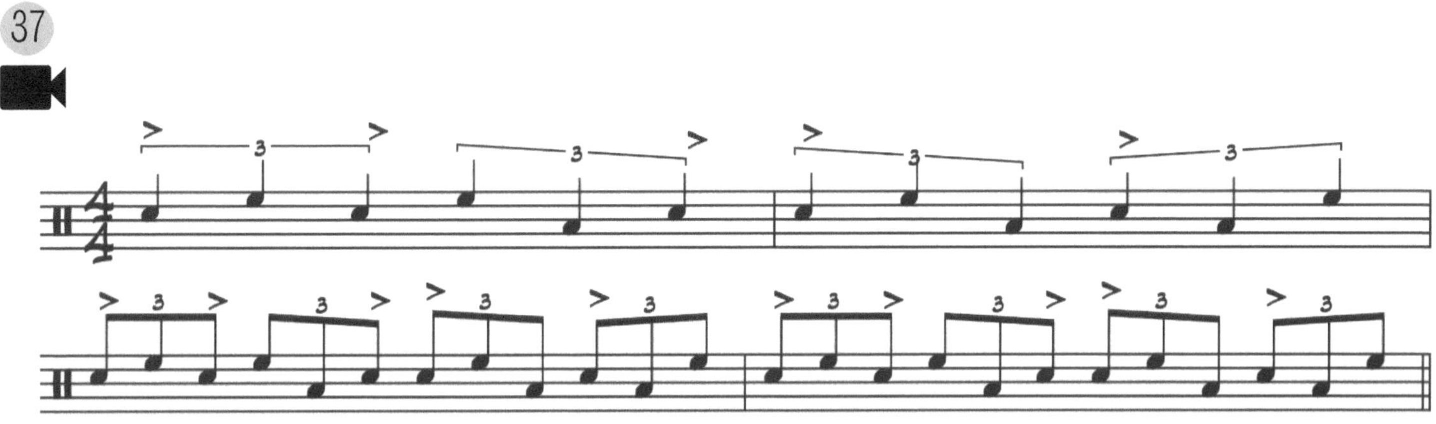

41

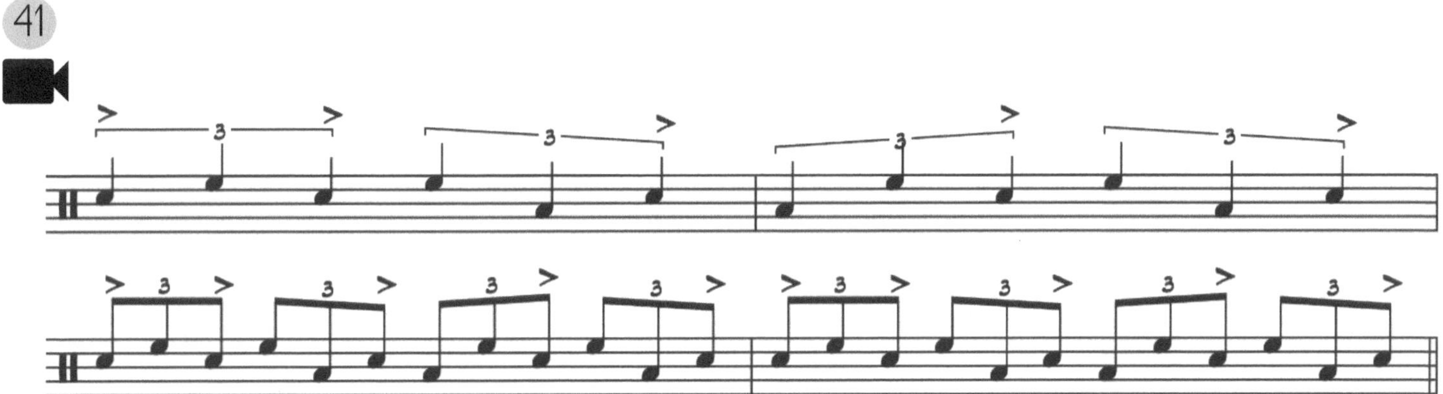

Moving With Inverted Paradiddle - Pages 50 - 52

Using pages 50-52, interpret each sixteenth note grouping as the Inverted Paradiddle. Use the previous format established with the Accents to Toms and Accents on Snare. Here are a few examples:

Page 50

4

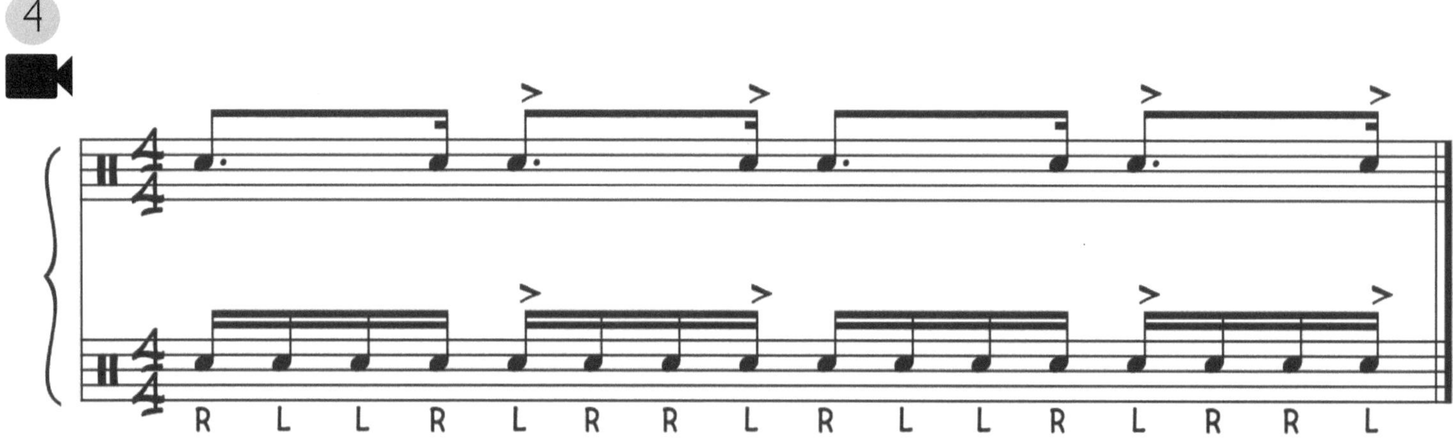

11

Page 51

16

23

Page 52

28

Bruce and David Garibaldi

Bruce with Glen Sobel (Left) and Matt Garstka (Middle)

Moving Accents to Toms

Page 50

4

11

Page 51

16

Moving Accents to Snare

Page 50

4

11

Page 51

16

Combining Inverted Paradiddle & Moving With Triplets: A Deeper Dive

Now that the last 2 systems have been processed, let's combine the Quarter note Triplets, 8th note Triplets and Inverted Paradiddle. The following examples will give insight into the usage of these rhythmic figures. Using pages 34 - 45 you can build fluidity while gaining a deeper understanding of shifting subdivisions. Here are a few from Pages 34 & 35–accents to Toms:

Page 34

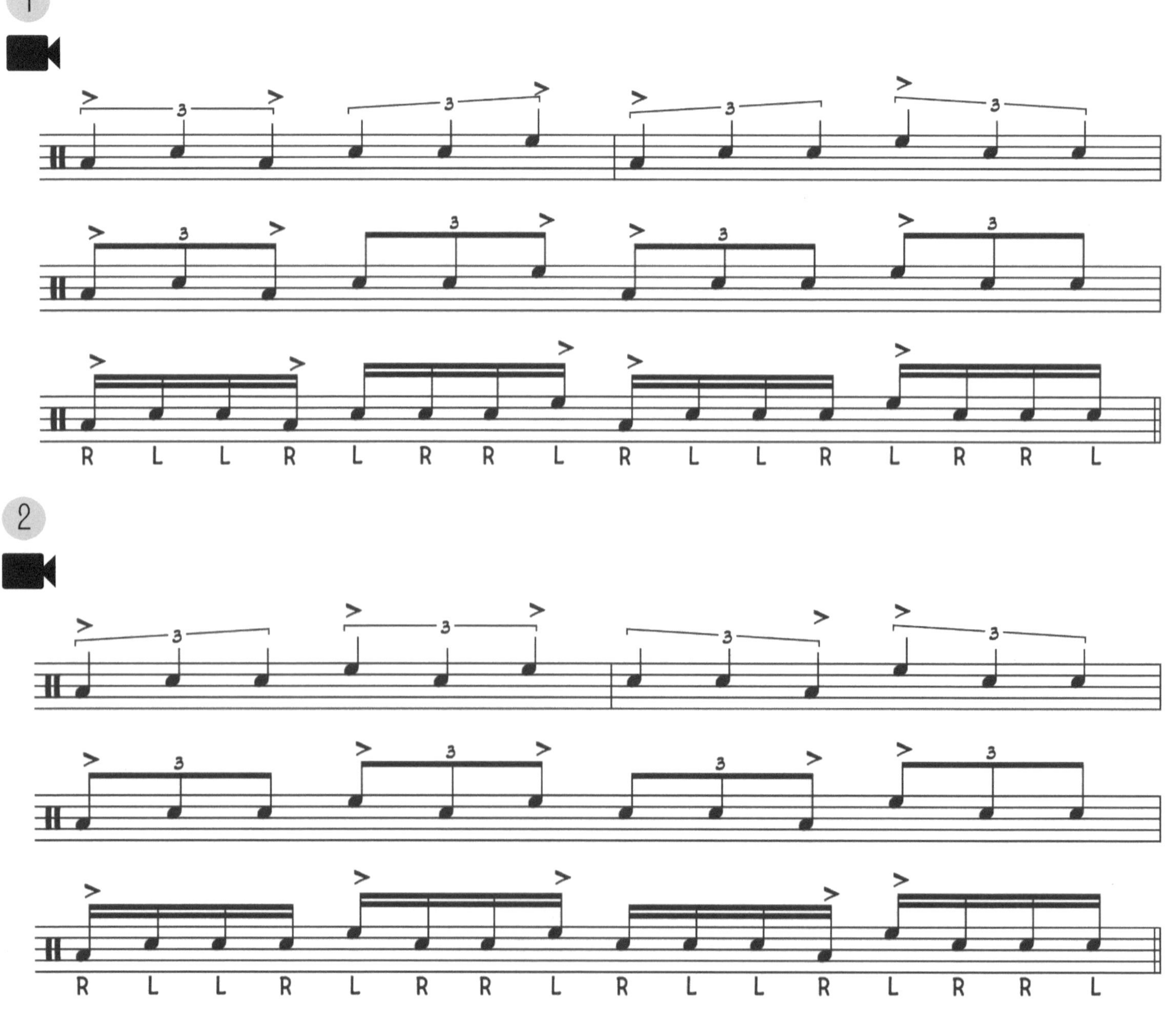

Moving Accents to Snare

Page 34

1

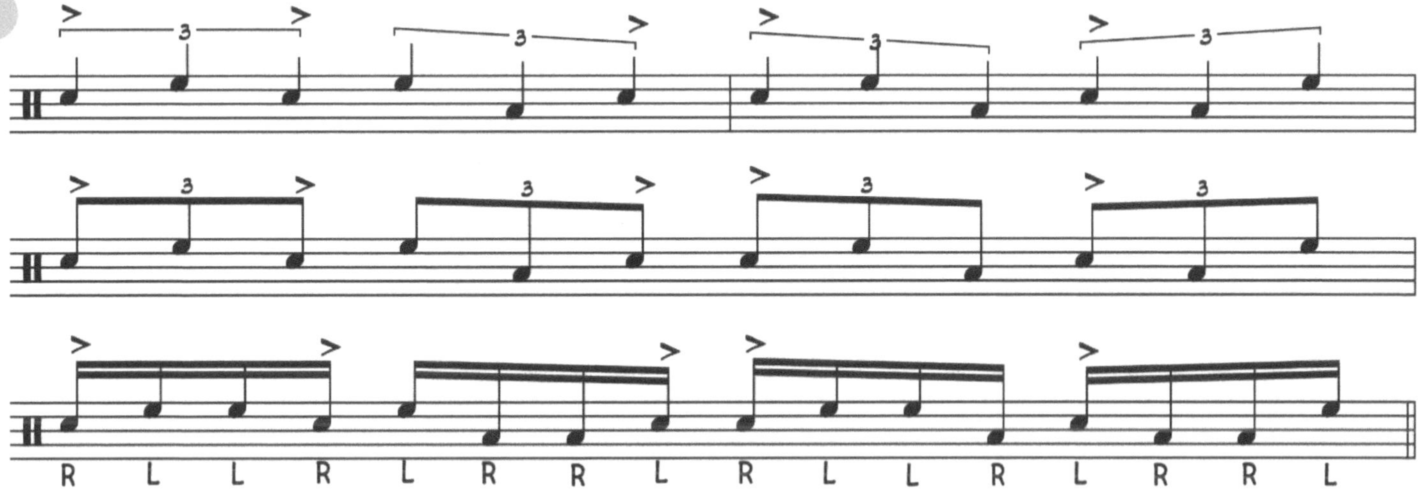
3
R L L R L R R L R L L R L R R L

2

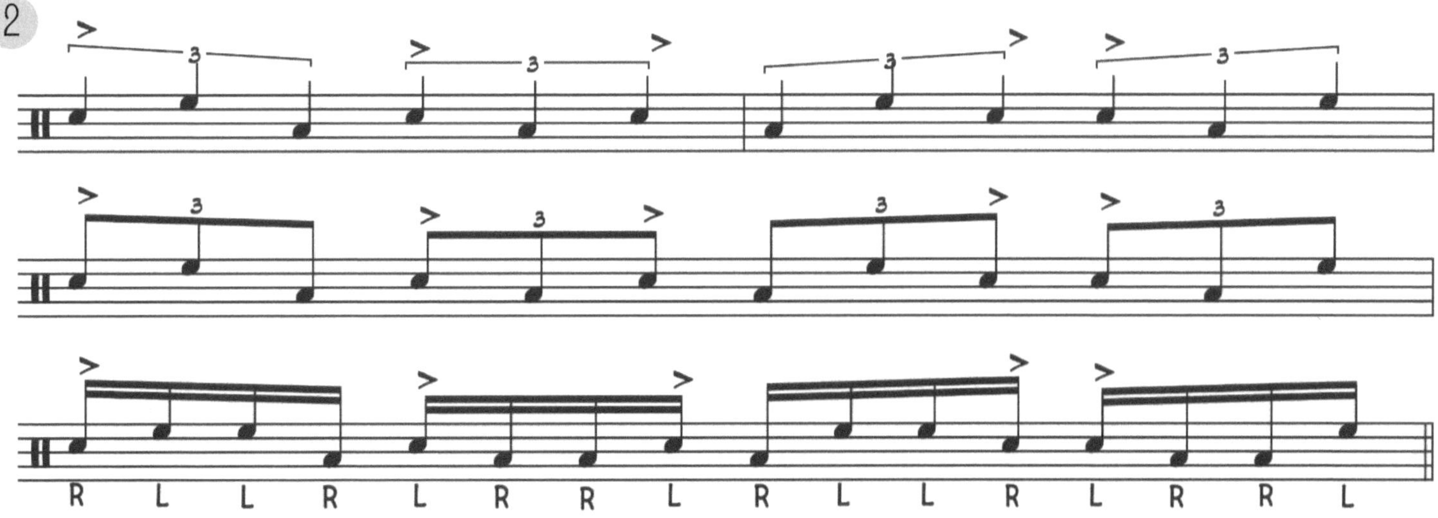
3
R L L R L R R L R L L R L R R L

Page 35

15

3
R L L R L R R L R L L R L R R L

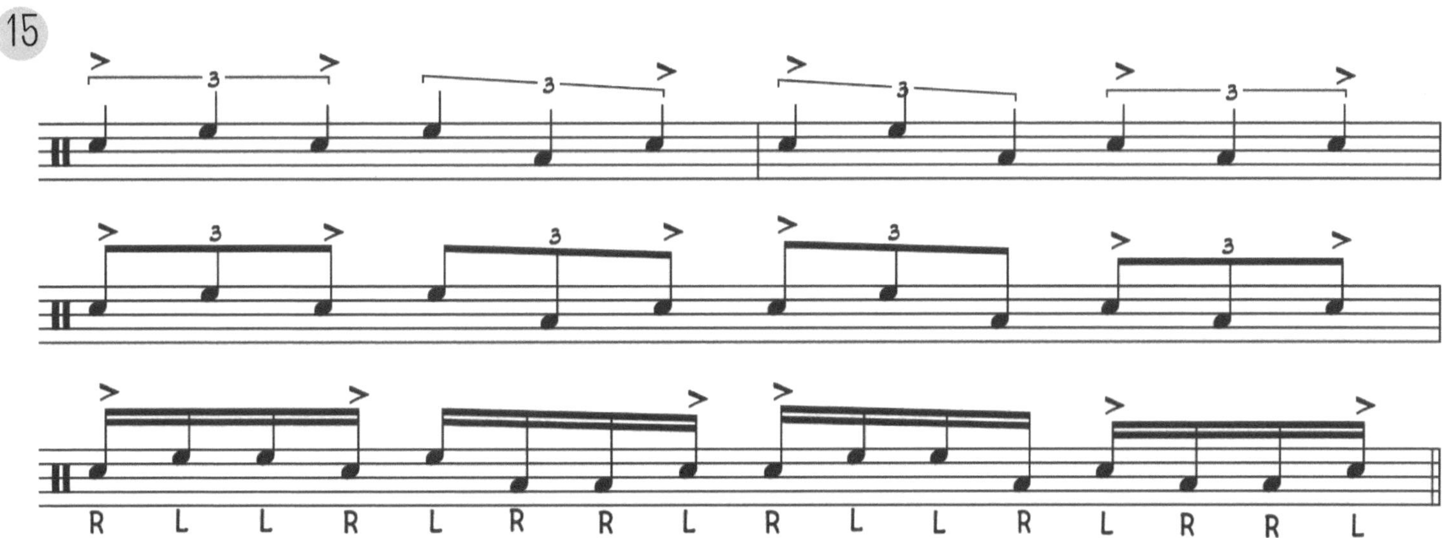

Accents to Cymbals with BD

This next approach will up the level of movement building upon an easy relationship to the cymbal and cymbal placement. Ergonomics and logic of cymbal placement should be a key consideration! First play the accents to Cymbals supported with the Bass drum and the unaccented notes on the Snare. When playing to the Cymbals bring a quality of touch and play to tips of the stick. This will present a challenge of placement as well as independence. Be sure your foot is synchronized with the accents. Here are some examples:

Page 34

1

Accents to Cymbals with BD Unaccented Notes Around The Set

The 2nd approach will be to play the unaccented notes around the kit. The unaccented notes on beat 1= Snare, beat 2= Small Tom, beat 3 = Snare and beat 4=Floor Tom. This should spotlight some movement challenges. There are other movement choices/combinations that can be applied. Start here and then add your ideas.

Page 34

1

A Deeper Dive: 5 Subdivisions

This next idea is intended to really spotlight range of movement and rhythmically modulate to accommodate the accuracy and fluidity of these moves. The Choreography of the Quarter Note Triplets will really open the clarity and fluidity of your movement. This will slowly contract as you move through each subdivision. In order to keep the Melody to 12 Notes the rhythmic flow requires a couple time signature adjustments. The arrangement will move as follows: from Quarter Note Triplets in 4/4 to 8th Notes in 6/4 to 8th Note Triplets in 4/4 to 16ths in 3/4 and finally 16th Note Triplets in 4/4 (hang on to your hat!). My thoughts on these rests more in concept rather than content. Meaning I only use a few exercises.

Page 34

A Super Deep Dive

Take the Accents on the Snare and play the unaccented notes on the Cymbals with the BD.
There are 3 systems that I use.
<u>Note: All Triplets AND 16ths to be played with alternating strokes.</u>

First Interpret as 8th Note Triplets. Examples:

Page 34

1

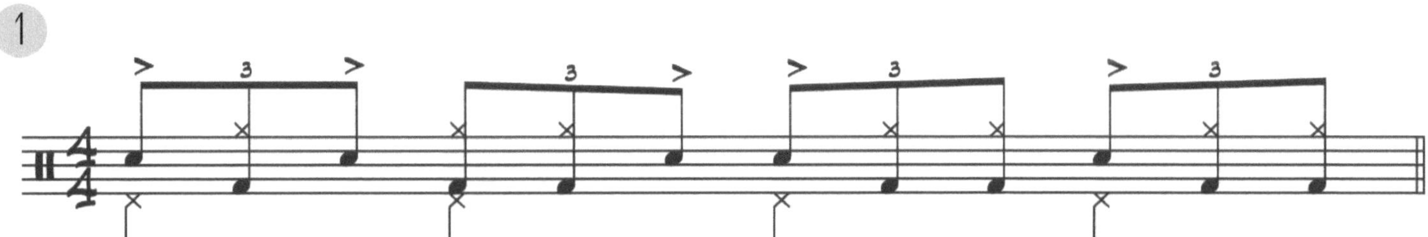

Then modulating the Triplet phrase to 16ths in 3/4. (Maintain hi-hat on quarter notes)

2

Melodies: Play the RH on the Floor Tom and the Left Hand on the Small Tom

Page 34

5

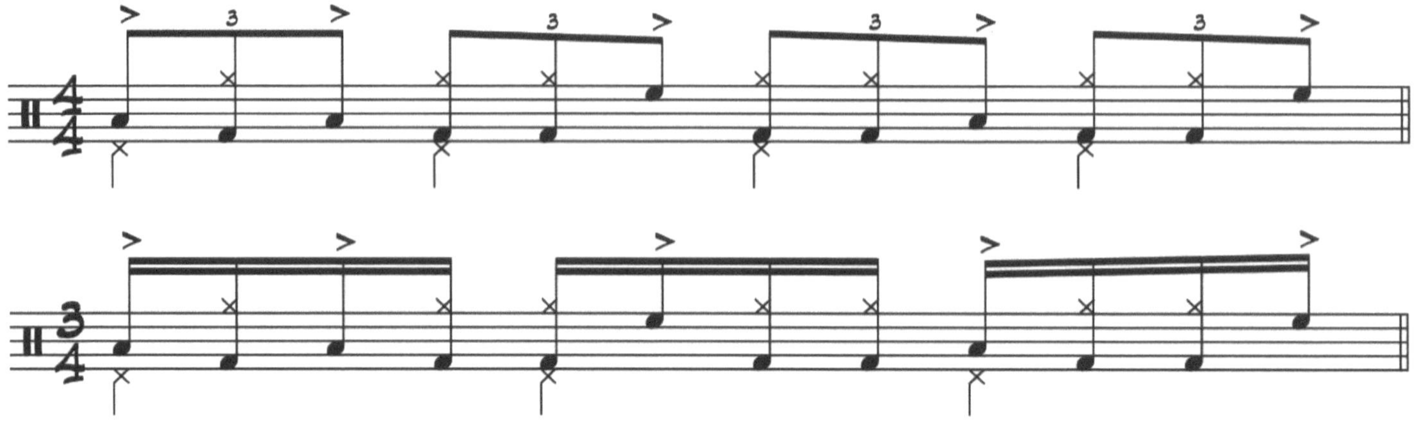

15

Bruce at PASIC

Moving With Doubles

This concept was adapted to find some nuance and interpretation to the idea of adding doubles around the Triplet based Melodies inspired by Jack DeJohnette. Rather than staying in a mathematical alignment within the Triplets, I use a method that includes Quintuplets to add a more round effect to the idea.

Setting Up the Movement with Doubles

These first eight exercises build a familiarity with quintuplets, sextuplets, and dotted sixteenth note groupings and are designed to build an expansion and contraction from the Quintuplet to the Sextuplet and vice versa. This gives an elastic Feel to the time. Find the subtlety and nuance to these.

D

E

F

And finally, these are set up to find a place for the double to not be registered in a mathematical approach but not an Inverted paradiddle either—there is that in between feel that will take time to process. Look at the Outline melody as the crust of the pie and the doubles are to be filled in and accommodate the shape of the crust.

G

H

Apply to:

Page 34

1

2

Apply to:

Page 37

43

47

Moving Accents to Toms

Now, let's move these accents to the toms:

Apply to:

Page 34

Page 37

Moving Accents to Snare

Page 34

Page 37

Accents to Cymbals with BD

Page 34

1

Page 37

47

Accents to Cymbals with BD Unaccented Notes Around The Set

Page 34

1

Page 37

47

Accents/Moving With Paradiddles

Using pages 47-49 take the 8th notes and apply the Single Paradiddle starting on the pad to get the flavor of the Accents and how they play into the Single Paradiddle sticking. Once the feel for the accents is established move the Accents to the Toms.

Page 47

Now, let's move the accents to the toms.

Page 48

Ostinato

The following exercises are inspired by Terry Bozzio. These are to set up a nice balance of melody as well as independence.

Ostinato with Triplets

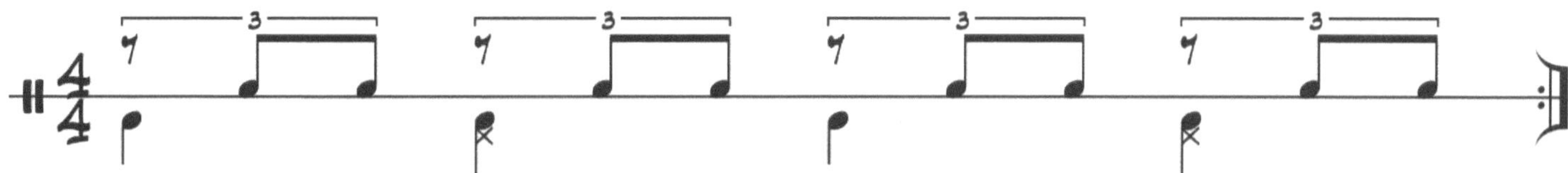

a. Left hand plays ostinato on small tom

b. Right hand plays melody on floor tom

Apply to:

Page 34

Page 35

a. Right hand plays ostinato on floor tom

b. Left hand plays melody on small tom

Apply to:

Page 34

1

Page 35

13

Ostinato with Straight Eighths in Cut Time

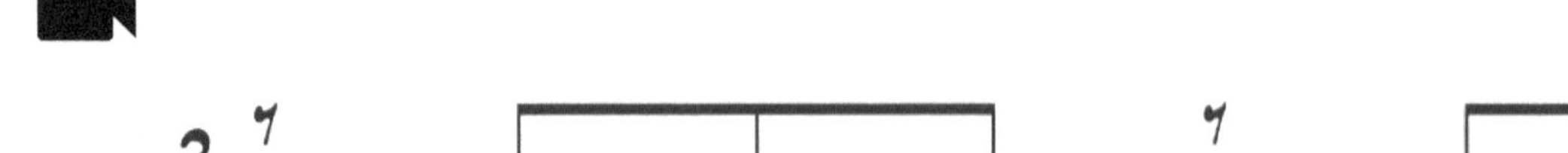

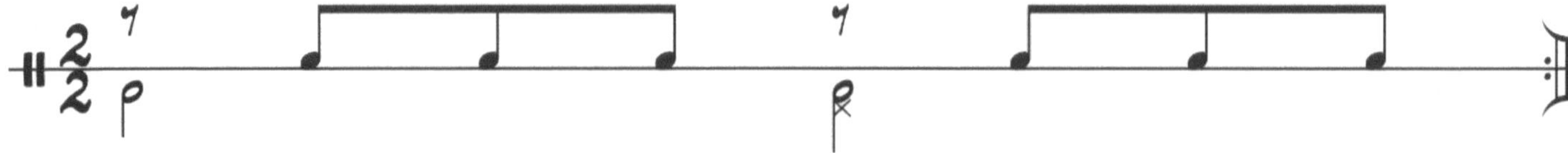

a. Left hand plays ostinato on small tom

b. Right hand plays melody on floor tom

Apply to:

Page 34

3

Similar to Ostinato with Triplets, also play these exercises as follows:

a. Right hand plays ostinato on floor tom

b. Left hand plays melody on small tom

Ostinato Warm-ups Chart

The Chart on the following page contains additional ostinato exercises within both the Triplet and Cut Time subdivisions. The chart also contains more advanced melodies to try. Utilize the same steps from the previous ostinato exercises in this book.

Ostinato Warm-ups

Ostinato Triplet:

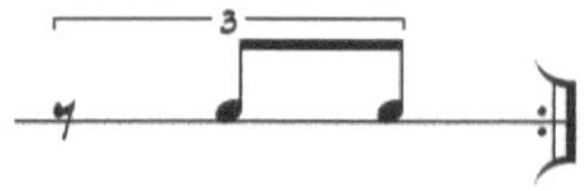

Melodies:

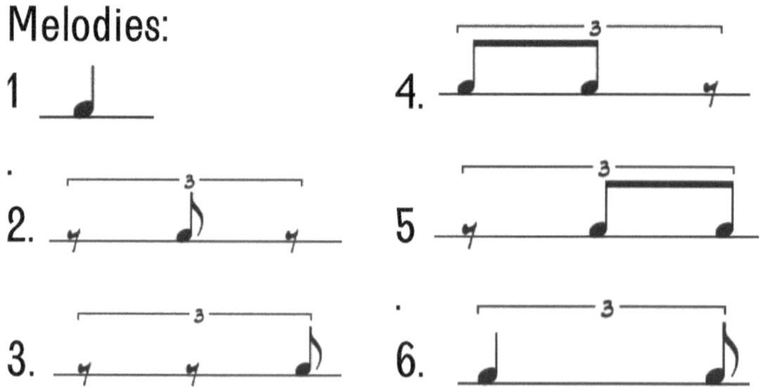

1

2.

3.

4.

5

6.

Advanced:

7.

8.

9.

10.

11.

12.

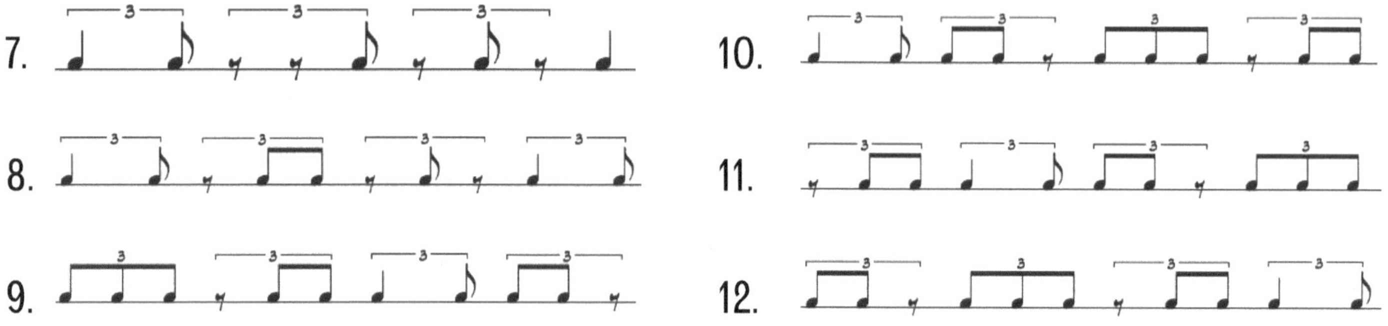

16ths or 8ths (Cut time)

Ostinato:

Melodies:

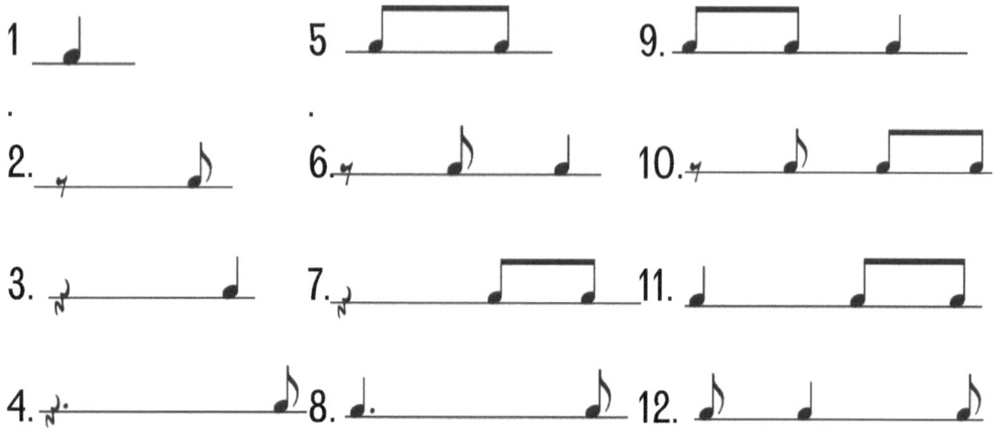

1

2.

3.

4.

5

6.

7.

8.

9.

10.

11.

12.

Advanced:

13.

14.

15.

16.

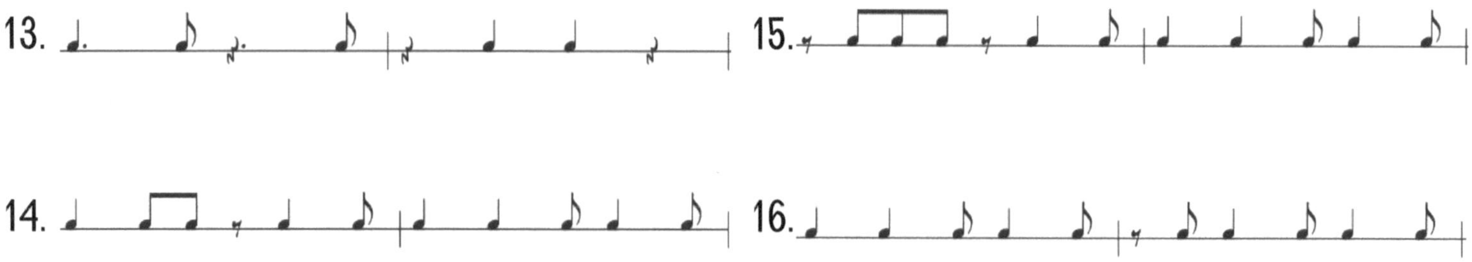

EPILOGUE: Reflections

As you can ascertain from diving into this book the ideas are endless. In reflecting back on my studies as well as my 40 years of teaching, these concepts have been immensely helpful in putting forward the concept of Flow. I hope you will benefit and gain some Mastery of Flow and improve your skills to become a better Musician.

A Young Bruce On His Ludwigs